Everybody's
Favorite

Everybody's Favorite

TALES FROM THE WORLD'S WORST PERFECTIONIST

Lillian Stone

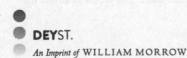

DEYST.

An Imprint of WILLIAM MORROW

● ●
● **DEY**ST.

FIRST EDITION

Designed by Jennifer Chung

Library of Congress Cataloging-in-Publication Data has been applied for.

ISBN 978-0-06-324103-9

23 24 25 26 27 LBC 5 4 3 2 1

 For her

Contents

Everybody's
Favorite

Attack of the Madisons

If the pen is mightier than the sword, then to ten-year-old girls in 2004, the gel pen was mightier than a flame-throwing bazooka. Gel pens, if you remember them, were the most sacred of instruments. The nib was precise; the iridescent ink flowed silkily onto the page, adorning dollar-store composition books with Gutenberg-level flair. The colors ranged from prim, reserved pink to bold, opulent silver that lent itself beautifully to fancy correspondence. More formal than a mechanical pencil, classier than the philistine BIC pens wielded by hicks and hayseeds, gel pens weren't to be wasted on schoolwork. They were saved for communication with one's crush ("DO U LIKE ME EVEN THOUGH I FELL OFF THE MONKEY BARS AND SCREAMED IN AGONY CHECK YES OR NO"), fifth-grade Student Council election propaganda ("A VOTE 4 LILLIAN IS A VOTE 4 UNFETTERED FRUIT SNACK ACCESS"), or emergency projectile implementation if you saw a weird bug.

Gel pens weren't invented until the mid-eighties. Still, think of how they might've jazzed up historical documents had they dawned in an earlier era. Imagine if the Founding Fathers had asserted man's inalienable rights in bubble gum–scented gel ink. Think of a weeping medieval peasant scanning a list of Black Plague victims penned in glittery turquoise bubble letters alongside a doodle that reads "LY-LAS: LUV YA LIKE A SISTER." Regardless, for me, gel pens were best used when writing lists. As an obsessive-compulsive ten-year-old, I clung to lists: lists of friends, lists of enemies, lists of my favorite and least favorite snacks, lists of things that could kill me ("WASP AT-TACK, SHARK ATTACK, BECOMING ENGULFED IN FLAMES WHILE RIDING RAZOR SCOOTER AT HIGH SPEEDS, STRAY COCONUT, DE-SPAIR/ANGUISH"). Lists helped me organize my short-circuiting brain, as well as my fifth-grade obligations. The latter were few, as I represented the near bottom of the Disney Elementary School social hierarchy. (Located in the Missouri Ozarks, the school's connec-tion to Walt Disney was unclear, made even more confusing by our mascot: the dolphin, perhaps the furthest evolutionary link from Mickey Mouse.) For context, my cooler peers spent their summers competing in outdoor swim leagues or camping with their families. I spent my breaks volunteering at a nearby horse ranch called the Branderosa, though I was deemed too clumsy for high-stakes volun-teer jobs like brushing horses' tails.

Of course, this was 2004, and I wasn't the only one with a short-circuiting brain. The early 2000s sank the Western world into a dis-organized, frenzied, pre-tech identity crisis. We knew something was coming—MySpace had just broken one million unique visitors per month; a sentient wax aardvark named Mark Zuckerberg had just launched a website for people who hate women. In those days, Americans had two choices: turn to hyperpatriotic activities in vague support of the Iraq War (tying ribbons around trees, applaud-ing airport racism), or trawl issues of *Us Weekly* to determine Chris-tina Aguilera's exact waist circumference. Society was sandwiched between the cocaine-fueled ghoulishness of the nineties and the Kardashian buttock frenzy of the 2010s, and no one was entirely sure how to proceed. So we turned to lists like these, published in big, bold tabloid fonts:

- The Sexiest Men Alive
- Celebrities Who Didn't Seem Excited Enough About the American Flag Last Week

- Items in Nicole Richie's Extraordinarily Small Purse
- Master Cleanse Side Effects, Ranked by Odor
- Low-Carb Bread Alternatives That Taste the Least Like Petroleum
- Everything Wrong with Hilary Duff
- Everything Wrong with Britney Spears
- Everything Wrong with Jessica Simpson
- Reasons Jared Fogle Seems Like a Trustworthy Guy

At some point, I became obsessed with these lists—especially the ones that involved picking apart young blondes. I suckled thoughtfully on my pink glitter retainer and relished the idea that a human's flaws could be so neatly presented, packaged in a way that made self-improvement a step-by-step directive. This appealed to me because, in 2004, I was on the cusp of puberty, preparing to plunge into a lifetime of deep, sweaty self-hatred. I could hear the shame coming for me. It slunk into my bedroom at night and taunted me beneath the shadow of my Orlando Bloom poster. In my mind, pubescent self-loathing was shaped like a Nelly Furtado backup dancer, a long-haired metaphor rocking a three-inch waist, a bejeweled belly chain, a pocket full of Lancôme Juicy Tube lip gloss, and the removable feet of a Bratz doll. We'll call her Madison.

Madison was a manifestation of my adolescent anxiety, a phantom formed by everything I'd never be. Until she began her reign of terror, I had no idea anything was wrong with me. I spent most of my childhood stomping around my native Ozark hills in a pair of glittery pink jelly sandals, scowling at my younger siblings and frying my eyeballs in front of my family's fuzzy TV set. I was odd, clumsy, and cursed with premature horniness, yes—but I was too busy sounding out sex scenes from my grandmother's trashy novel collection to realize that I was a social late bloomer. I thought I was doing just fine.

But Madison still struck, the product of my rapidly spiking hormones and early 2000s tabloid consumption. One day, I was belly flopping into the neighborhood pool in my best imitation of Macho Man Randy Savage; the next, I was overcome with anxiety, characterized by a sudden slap of self-consciousness. I had become instantly beholden to Madison's spectral insistence that I was the most pathetic preteen girl to ever skulk through the aisles of rue21. I was wrong. I was bad. I was weird. I was *musky*.

Madison stuck around from that point on. She raised an eyebrow as I went for a second helping of Shake 'n Bake at dinner. She shook her head, wagged her finger, and smiled menacingly as I considered striking up a conversation with my crush. She spit on me during a particularly grueling gym class that involved running until your shorts fell off or you passed out. Madison never said a word, but her message was clear: *Everything about you is wrong and gross, and everyone can tell.*

Fed up with Madison's tricks, I gave in. Inspired by *Us Weekly*, I unsheathed my gel pen to compose the ultimate list: Everything Wrong with Me. I decided this no-holds-barred list of personal failings would strip away my dull exterior, revealing my inner cool girl in all her puka-shell-wearing glory. I wanted to transform, and outlining my most egregious flaws in glittery gel ink seemed like the best way to do it. With this comprehensive list of Reasons I Sucked Major Ass spread before me, I could systematically work away at each issue. I'd tick off imperfections until I was a new woman. Specifically, a woman with a spiky-haired boyfriend, a Pottery Barn Teen loft bed, a standing offer to join Y2K girl group B*Witched, and the spiritual fortitude to shop among the giant half-naked decals at Abercrombie & Fitch without running out screaming "MEN'S NIPPLES!!!"

Unlike Madison, The List wasn't metaphorical. The List was real, penned in the front cover of a wide-rule composition book. It was all-encompassing, addressing a vast array of concerns, ranging from my cavernous pores to my social ineptitude to a very specific affliction I have since dubbed Resting Caveman Face Syndrome, the unfortunate result of the hulking, adult-sized forehead that overwhelmed the rest of my as-yet immature features.

Most of the concerns addressed in The List were resolved after I grew into my forehead. But here's the rub: I still carry it with me. Not the literal List—that's lost to history, along with my gel pens—but the aftertaste. I've outgrown most of the issues presented in the original List; still, sometimes, if I squint, it's like I can see sinister messages scrawled in glitter across my bedroom wall. It's Madison, the sexy demon of my prepubescent dreams. She's reminding me that she's still around, perhaps waiting for the few days during my menstrual cycle during which I feel like the ugliest freak bitch on earth. "Pores still gaping, I see," she scribbles across my forehead, dotting her *i*'s with little hearts and adjusting her belly chain.

Most of the time, I know how to shut her up. "Can it," I'll mutter, examining my face in the mirror before going about my day as a generally functional woman. I'll ignore her giggles as I sit at my desk, outlining my grocery list in practical black ballpoint ink. But some days, when the moon is full and the teens outside don their secondhand Juicy Couture sweatsuits, I feel a curious chill in the air. It's as though Madison's bony, spray-tanned hand is gripping mine as I scrawl out whatever messy thought is rattling around in my noggin that day.

The pursuit of perfection is exhausting, though it starts innocently enough. At ten, my preoccupations were mainly aesthetic; I wanted to minimize my forehead, tweeze my eyebrows, and overhaul my wardrobe with spare Kohl's Cash. But as I grew, so, too, did my list of people to please. Real people—not sexy metaphors like Madison. The closer I got to adulthood, the more I struggled to contort myself into the perfect friend, the perfect love interest, the perfect daughter, the perfect dog owner, the perfect employee.

I found that the act of contorting oneself is like crossing your eyes: Do it for too long, and you'll get stuck that way.

Ideally, I'd look back on The List as a low-stakes childhood relic. It's great comedy fodder, like the romantic poem I once dedicated to the entire male cast of *Lord of the Rings: Return of the King*. But I see it more as a harbinger of things to come. The List marked the beginning of a lifetime of bending myself into uncomfortable shapes for someone else's benefit. The tendency is partially genetic; I come from a long line of neurotics who chase pills with sixers of Rolling Rock in an attempt to dull the embarrassment of human existence. The tendency is also systemic. To be a woman is to withstand a midwestern hailstorm of criticism. Strangers line up to nitpick everything from the timbre of your voice to the length of your toes. (Too long, and you're a Finger Toe; too short, and you risk displeasing the discerning gentlemen of wikiFeet.)

It's never been worse, this public nitpickery. Madison's 2004 demands were nothing compared to the round-the-clock hellscape that is the internet. I'd take the nasty tabloid headlines of the early 2000s in a heartbeat if it meant I never had to see a shiny-haired woman boasting about radical authenticity on social media. You're telling me that it's no longer enough to love myself—I also have to *sell* the act of loving myself? You're telling me that I still have to comply with the same tired beauty and behavior standards, but now I have to convince strangers that I've done so with *no effort at all*? You're telling me that my life has to be one never-ending parade of radical self-adoration in a public forum where I will inevitably receive death threats for expressing an opinion about breakfast cereal? And I have to do it all while grinning broadly, having an awesome time, and very publicly listening to the exact kind of music that everyone I've ever met in my life will find pleasing? Great. Glad we're on the same page.

That's where Madison comes back in. The truth is that this isn't just my book; it's hers, too. I guess that's to be expected, since I still haven't figured out how to banish her for good. Sometimes, I still feel the urge to chip away at unsavory bits of myself the way you'd hammer zebra barnacles from a swaying dock. The problem is my personal history of letting others determine which bits are worth hammering. To bend to the ruthless expectations of others is to shift, chameleonic, between identities until nothing particularly interesting remains. You become everybody and nobody all at once. It's like that tired old line "Who am I? I'm whoever you want me to be, baby."

Some days, I feel like I'm chasing Madison around my room with a butterfly net. She skitters from corner to corner like a house centipede, flipping me the bird with one perfectly rectangular middle fingernail. God, she's fast. But I take heart knowing that everyone—especially those who experienced the unique cruelty of early 2000s girlhood—harbors their own Madison. Every girl who grew up sandblasting her face with St. Ives Apricot Scrub also battles a little voice in her head—a Madison voice—constantly listing the ways she could improve.

Will we ever banish those belly-chain-clad imaginary foes? No, I don't think so. We're too far gone. But I do think there's power in banding together and talking openly about all the ways we've tried to change ourselves. To poke fun at the ways society demands we bow and bend and scrape is to weaken the Madisons just a little bit. There's freedom in it. No, maybe *freedom* is too strong a word. Respite, more like. A little bit of room to breathe, as if you've loosened your studded Hot Topic belt and dropped all pretense and forgotten whether you're supposed to love yourself or hate yourself in this particular moment. We might not be able to banish the Madisons forever, but we *can* blare B*Witched and sing along at the top of our lungs. I found a club remix of "C'est La Vie" on YouTube. It plays on a loop for twenty hours. That should drown 'em out.

Nothing's Funnier Than Naked

I was five the first time I felt weird about my boobs. I was entertaining new friends, a pair of sporty twins named David and Eric who had shared a womb and a knack for Nerf warfare. We had spent the day at my place, throwing sticks at each other, riding couch cushions down the basement stairs, and trying to lasso the refrigerator with a jump rope. I didn't have many friends who were boys, and I leapt at the chance for a rough-and-tumble playdate fueled by Minute Maid concentrate.

By the time their mother arrived to pick them up, the three of us formed one overlapping mass, roly-poly limbs intertwined like a trio of baby orangutans, exhausted from playing a game that involved turning off all the lights and spinning in circles until you fell down or barfed a little. We struggled to keep our eyes open as we lay on my parents' frayed green living room couch, the tattered realm of our shifty-eyed cat, Bo-Peep.

"Bring the boys over any time," my mom gushed, straightening her AC/DC T-shirt and discreetly kicking a maimed Cabbage Patch doll under the couch. I can't remember exactly what we did to the doll, but I have to imagine it was Black Dahlia–esque.

The boys' mom folded her hands primly. "They do seem to have a good time together," she granted, watching warily as I stuck my fingers in my ears and flap-flap-flapped my tongue at the boys.

I'm not sure what happened next. My mom tells me that I darted away without excusing myself; I seem to remember making a big production out of leaving the room, marching away like a majorette. Either way, I left our guests in the living room, went to my bedroom down the hall, gently closed the door, and got completely naked.

Off went the pastel orange shorts that left a slight indent on my plump belly. Off went the purple tank top and the jelly sandals. Off went the floral underpants. I then tiptoed down the hall in the nude, waited for a lull in the moms' conversation, raised my hands above my head, uttered a primal scream, and streaked across the living room.

The streaking was meant as a joke—the ultimate comedic send-off after a day of unruly play. My guests and I had spent the day picking our noses, scratching our armpits, and jabbering nonsense at one another. To me, sprinting across the living room seemed like the perfect farewell for my new playmates. You send birthday party guests home with a bag of cheap party favors; you send wedding guests home with leftover cake or a flower arrangement. It stood to reason that I'd send David and Eric home with a hearty laugh inspired by my jiggling kid ass.

My guests were not amused. My mom clapped her hand over her mouth to stifle a hoot, but she's hardly a judge of good comedy. My mom is the kind of person who laughs in uncomfortable situations, like the time she accidentally drove over my friend's foot in the family sedan. Instead of responding like a normal, sympathetic person in that situation, my mom erupted into an involuntary giggle fit as my friend rocked back and forth, cradling her ankle and moaning in pain.

Because I was committed to entertaining my audience, I streaked again. I ran to the other side of the room and turned my back to the boys. I made the funniest sounds I could think of, screeching gibberish as I wiggled my butt *Coyote Ugly*–style. "HOO-HA! HOO-HA! HEE-OO!" I grunted, circling my hips and performing a series of deep knee bends.

The boys stared at me, wide-eyed and silent. Their mother stared at my mother, whose shoulders were now shaking hysterically. "Well, I think we'd better get going," their mother huffed, wrapping her arms protectively around the twins as they ogled my jazzy display. They left without another word, at which point my mother doubled over and laughed harder than she had during the *Challenger* explosion.

That's my first memory of bodily embarrassment. Before that day, I regularly frolicked in the buff, relishing my status as the proud child of a Naked Family. Please know that a Naked Family is not the same thing as a nudist family. Nudist families engage in nude grilling and nude lawn darts and nude movie nights as a matter of principle; a Naked Family bonds over the mutual understanding that bodies are weird, gross, very funny—and, thus, nothing to be particularly ashamed of. In my family, nothing's funnier than naked. My dad mooned us throughout my childhood, flashing the large submarine-shaped mole on the northeast quadrant of his right butt cheek. My mom and I made up a bathtime song called "Wash That Stanky Thang" that involved a series of obscene nude gyrations. My little brother and I performed nude vaudeville shows in the living room, me in a neon green mohawk wig pulled from the Halloween closet, him in a large polka-dot bow. These shows always ended with us sprinting out of the room, smacking our own butts, and cackling like hyenas. The shows went on until I was seven or eight; the incriminating Polaroids remain.

My family's fascination with bodily weirdness extends to the auditory realm. Family road trips became a test of human endurance as my siblings and I took turns filling the backseat with clouds of Dorito-fueled flatulence. Once I hit puberty, I'd lie on the couch and practice my armpit farts, which had a rich, tonal quality thanks to my hormonal pits. My dad would pass me en route to the kitchen. "Nice one," he'd say, grabbing a bag of Tostitos and releasing a tiny whisper of a fart. "Nice one," I'd reply, cupping my underarm to crank out a few more salutatory honkers. To this day, my dad still rips record-breaking blasters at the dinner table, which emit a thunderous *crack* as they ricochet off my parents' wooden dining chairs. At that point, he tilts his head down, pupils pointed coquettishly upward in his best Betty Boop, as if to say, "Aren't I cute?"

It should come as no surprise, then, that I decided to sprint naked in front of my two new pals. I was raised by a family of clowns who, in lieu of puppets and rubber chickens, prefer to entertain with their God-given assets. That's why I was so taken aback when the twins failed to see the comedy in my routine. In a way, it was my first time bombing onstage. I couldn't make 'em laugh, and I was horrified.

In hindsight, my shame was healthy. There comes a time in every girl's life when she must put away childish things, like unabashed nudity and uninvited gyrations. It's not that I had much to be ashamed of; there was nothing sexual about the streaking. My boobs weren't even boobs yet, just two puffy dots that hovered over my sternum. But the shame was there. I knew immediately that I had done something weird—pervy, even—and I was humiliated. Like Eve, I ate from the tree of knowledge, realized I was naked, and felt like a big creep.

As I got older, I realized that my family's approach to anatomical humor was pretty rare. Sure, I connected with a few disgusting compatriots. Around the time of the streaking incident, my friend Jeannette and I invented a crotch-inspecting game called Bathtub. During Bathtub, we'd lock ourselves in the bathroom and strip naked. "You girls okay in there?" her mom called. "Fine!" we'd scream, gleefully positioning ourselves in the bathtub for the express purpose of examining each other's genitals. I'd lie back in the bathtub while Jeannette waddled across the tub's edge, walking directly over me like a nude Godzilla. "HEY, NICE," I'd cry as Jeannette hovered above my face. "LOOKS JUST LIKE MINE!"

Then, we'd switch, giving Jeannette the opportunity to gaze up into my crevices. "HEY, NICE," she'd crow. "MINE LOOKS LIKE THAT, TOO!" I'd pipe up from my perch, asking: "Can you see my guts?" She'd respond with a solemn nod: "Yes, I think so."

We repeated the game for the better part of a year, documenting our respective anatomies with the rigor of bespectacled clinical researchers. It was a strictly scientific exercise; our bodies were weird, and we were curious. But it was also a comfort to realize that she and I had mostly the same stuff. We managed to clock our slight differences—a stray fold here, a freckle there—with a frank neutrality. In that moment, we knew with utter certainty that there are no good bodies or bad bodies—just bodies, in all their weird, jiggling glory. *HEY, NICE!*

But as I approached puberty, most of my friends seemed actively dedicated to hiding their bodily weirdness. Not only did they fail to cut the cheese with any sort of vigor; they also went to extreme lengths to conceal their junk. At slumber parties, they'd scuttle into the bathroom to change into their pajamas; meanwhile, I'd throw off my clothes and crab-walk nude across the bedroom to get a laugh. My friends would creep to the darkest corners of the public pool locker room and take turns changing behind beach towels, pulled taut like airplane banner advertisements. "DON'T LOOK," they'd squeal as I stood there in my birthday suit, spread-eagled like the Vitruvian Man. I'd roll my eyes, stealing a line from my mom's playbook: "It's nothin' I haven't seen before."

Then came the Bra Times. I was resistant to wearing a bra for obvious reasons—bras are horrible—but my friends seemed to accept them with glee. This was especially true for my church friends, whose genteel southern mothers were militant about modesty. I first noticed it during a fifth-grade church lock-in. We sat in the car-

peted children's sanctuary, beading key chains to hand out to passing sinners, and my friend Maureen kept fidgeting with her pajama
top. I glanced over, annoyed. I had been deep in concentration ar-
ranging my beads in a vaguely Rastafarian pattern inspired by the
Bob Marley kiosk at the mall. "Why are you so fidgety?" I demanded.
She gave me a dirty look. "I'm just fixing my *bra*," she replied.

I wrinkled my nose, confused. "We're in our PJs," I said. "Why
are you wearing a bra with your PJs?"

She looked at me like I had a huge, throbbing breast growing out
of my forehead. "For *modesty*," she huffed in a tone that was becoming increasingly familiar. It was the same tone my other friends used
when scoffing at my unabashed nakedness. "Lillian," my friend Beth
said primly as I strode around her bedroom like Porky Pig, bare
from the waist down, "I *really* don't need to see that."

The more time I spent around my prepubescent peers, the more
left out I felt. It's as though they knew something I didn't. They were
united in their squeamishness about their bodies, strapped into
their racerback sports bras twenty-four hours a day, their tiny ski
slope boobs mashed against their torsos with viselike security. I
was fatally picky about fabrics and waistbands, so averse to discomfort that I spent most days in a threadbare pair of men's sweatpants. I couldn't—still can't—stand the feeling of being restricted
by clothing at night,* let alone something so torturous as a sports
bra. Even my subconscious was obsessed with comfort, a fact that
made me notorious for throwing off my pajamas in my sleep.

Eventually, I began to think that there was something baby-
ish about my relative lack of shame. I was still playing with dolls
and running around sans pants, even as my friends were poised
to enter the murky waters of menstruation. Around this time, a tall
girl named Charline stopped by for a playdate. I suggested that we
throw my Barbies a raucous rager, and she sniffed. "Maybe we could

---

* Yeah, PERVERTS, I sleep in the NUDE!!!

do something else," she said. "My doctor said I could start my period any day now." She didn't come out and say that we were too old for dolls. She didn't have to; her forthcoming menses suggested the end of our shared girlhood silliness. She, too, had embraced self-consciousness. She was approaching womanhood, something so secret and shameful that the word had to be whispered. I finally understood. Shame was a rite of passage, a mandatory mantle for anyone who wants to cross the threshold into the land of ultra-absorbent overnight pads and mystery discharge.

By the time I crossed that threshold, I knew roughly what to expect. My church sponsored a young women's retreat, where girls and their moms learned new and exciting ways to feel weird about our bodies. A mousy woman with an impossibly tight ponytail and a thick Louisiana accent taught us how to apply a light layer of Mary Kay eye shadow to our eyelids. I had lumped my eyeshadow on like Elvira, so heavy it weighed my eyelashes down. "Makeup is meant to enhance your natural, God-given beauty, girls," the woman said, striding across the church gym where the seminar took place. She bent down, patted my shoulder stiffly, and handed me a Q-tip. "Not cover it up." I stared at the Q-tip and blinked my goopy eyes. I thought about the garish red lipstick I had slicked on for all those nude vaudeville shows with my brother. I grabbed the Q-tip and dragged it across both eyelids.

Later that day, a frizzy-haired female gynecologist led a session called "Loving the Body God Created!" During the session, we were invited to sip lemonade, eat half-frozen eclairs, and watch the gynecologist unwrap a few enormous maxi pads. One by one, she peeled the pads off of their plastic backing and slapped them, sticky side down, on the wall behind her. "Panty liner, standard pad, heavy flow pad," she recited, pointing academically. I can't remember tampons ever being a part of this discussion, probably because of the lingering rumor among some of the snottier church moms that tampons compromised your virginity. At the end of the session, the organizers handed out complimentary coin purses meant to house our menstrual products. "No one has to know," said the woman with the Louisiana accent, winking as she handed me a purse.

It seemed that every conversation about puberty involved hiding it. My mom taught me to tie a jacket around my waist in case of bleeding breakthroughs. My friends and I crossed our knees and held our pee throughout the school day, afraid to use the bathroom for fear that someone would suspect something period-related was afoot. This was not the era of wet 'n' wild body acceptance. This was the era of looking shyly at one's nether regions with a compact mirror. We had no menstrual cup influencers or Instagram-famous gynecologists to follow; we had no clue if we were normal or not. We relied on the word of trashy magazines and the horrible boy in my class who once proclaimed that he could smell when we were on the rag. That day, I went home and slathered noxious Bath & Body Works Sweet Pea lotion over my labia. What followed was the sort of vaginal stinging that can only be described as Isengard-esque.

Slowly, I learned what my sheepish friends already knew to be true: that womanhood is all about smoke and mirrors. Boobs get strapped down under one's pajamas. Makeup gets applied, but only in secret. The normal machinations of one's body are to be hidden at all costs, even if that means burning your beaver with a thick layer of floral moisturizer. And while I still ripped the occasional armpit fart with my family, even they seemed to think that I had aged out of anatomical humor. One night, my dad and I sat rewatching *Dumb and Dumber* for the fiftieth time, laughing about frozen snot crystals and explosive diarrhea. "We got no food; we got no jobs," my dad quoted, tossing a tortilla chip into his mouth. "Our pets' HEADS ARE FALLIN' OFF," I replied, completing my family's most sacred call-and-response. Eyes glued to the screen, I absent-mindedly reached over to empty my backpack. Out tumbled my biology textbook, along with a handful of unopened tampons. My dad took one look at the tampons and turned beet red, taunting:

"Geh-*rossss*."

That settled it. My days of parading across the living room, proud of my body's weird bits, were over. My body had become a secret meant to be stashed away until it was time to open myself to the whims of adult male acceptability. The whole world had the power to make me feel weird about my boobs.

It wasn't until college that I started to settle into my body, leaning back into the slapstick humor of my youth. It's near impossible to hide your putrid habits in college, where you're surrounded by thousands of coeds clamoring over each other like crustaceans. My friends and I left thick, gritty films of hairspray on every surface of our respective dorm rooms, crafted elaborate hair mosaics on our shower walls, and propped our clammy bare feet up on coffee tables to watch bad sci-fi movies. We moved through the world in a foul haze, driven mad by hormones and wine coolers. As a kid, my siblings and I squeezed into the backseat of the car and tortured each other with farts; as a collegian, my classmates and I sardined ourselves into tiny, asbestos-ridden apartments, downing frozen margaritas and Cheez-Its. God, we were flammable.

College was the first time post-puberty that I had friends who were willing to laugh at their bodies. We didn't have much of a choice; we were crammed into close quarters, and we desperately needed one another as we tried to navigate the physical hurdles of young adulthood. We traded secrets, including my signature Spread-'N'-Rip-It technique. It's designed for when you're spooning with a love interest and you feel a fart burbling through your system. The mechanics are self-explanatory.

We also consulted on medical mysteries that circulated our campus like red, itchy wildfire. A few weeks into freshman year, one of my suitemates pulled me aside and dropped her pants. "I think I have chlamydia," she whimpered, pointing down to her inflamed crotch. She didn't have chlamydia; it was a yeast infection from wearing tight denim shorts on the Slip-'N'-Slide at freshman orientation. But at that moment, I knew we had dropped the pretense. If we were going to survive four years of sexual minefields and dismal nutrition, we'd have to ditch the shame.

Body shame is useless. It makes it impossible to figure yourself out; it's easy to mistake a Slip-'N'-Slide rash for chlamydia if you're too ashamed to ask questions. It's easy to confuse a frenzied clitoris-mashing session with carnal ecstasy when your sexual education is limited to church retreats and sneaky MTV viewings.

Body shame also makes it tough to be honest—with yourself, but also with others. When we buy into the idea that our bodies are gross and weird and not to be discussed, we lose opportunities to connect. We miss the chance to giggle with friends, crying out "You, too?!" We never learn how to tell partners that, no, I'm not into having my belly button licked, actually. We're robbed of opportunities to marvel at our own flesh, whether it be a source of romance and pride or a source of comedy. But when we finally get honest about our bodies—the good along with the gross, as if the two could possibly be assessed separately—we learn that there are no good bodies and no bad bodies; only bodies. All different, all normal. All gleefully disgusting.

I suppose the girls who strapped themselves into racerback sports bras made their mothers proud. They're all married now, with drab husbands and loud babies and shiplap houses. I don't have a drab husband or a loud baby or a shiplap house. I have an apartment packed with air freshener and Monistat suppositories and Body Glide for when my thighs rub together in the summer. My tampons sit right out on the bathroom sink. I write in front of a box fan, sweat pouring into my enormous faded Hanes value pack underpants. Sometimes I drink cheap white wine and strip off my clothes, streaking past the gilded mirror in my hallway to catch a glimpse of my jiggling flesh. There's nothing salacious about the jiggling; it's still just my dumb body. I have uneven boobs and puffy nipples and hair in weird places. I have cellulite that ripples across the backs of my thighs and lends itself beautifully to the slow-motion videos I send my foulest friends. The videos vary in content; sometimes I'll smack my own behind and holler "HA-CHA-CHA!" Other times, I'll zoom in on my boobs, bouncing up and down on my toes so they spin in circles like fleshy helicopters.

More often than not, my friends send one back. I've made a few new girlfriends since college, all of whom like to laugh at their dumb bodies. When we're old, we'll all sit topless in lawn chairs, fanning ourselves in the summer heat and complaining about all the creakings and crunchings that come with an aging body. We'll tweeze our chin hairs and laugh at how our expanding ripples of flesh slap together when we get up to get another glass of lemonade. When everyone leaves, I'll stand in front of the bathroom mirror and hoist one sagging breast into the air, then the other, letting them fall with a hearty *slap*. My family had the right idea all along. There really is nothing funnier than naked.

Popular Sins, Explained

A brief and rigorously researched primer for those unfamiliar with the taxonomy of sin.

G reed is one of the most popular sins, which explains why it inspired so many Bible verses. For example, Luke 12:15, which reads "Life does not consist in an abundance of possessions" and was clearly written in a time before pinball machines and dirt bikes.

Cussing is a confusing sin, because it requires context. When a farmer refers to his donkey as an ass, that is not a cuss. When a farmer refers to his donkey as a piss-soaked fuck trumpet that crawled out of Satan's rotten shithole, that is a cuss.

Biblical scholars define sloth as "the sinful desire for ease." I define sloth as "long monkey."

Gluttony refers to all manner of overindulgence, including drunkenness, downing a trayful of Communion grape juice shooters, or eating too many stale Starbursts from the Vacation Bible School treasure chest and suffering a catastrophic sugar crash while reciting the Fruits of the Spirit.

Lust is what happens when the praise-band rhythm guitarist wears head-to-toe Billabong.

Peeing in the pastor's aboveground pool during the annual

youth group summer hootenanny is almost certainly a sin, but not a very popular one. I don't know anyone who would do that.

"Sins of the flesh" is a general term to describe squishing your boobs together and screaming "ALL ABOARD THE MANGO TRAIN!"

Wrath takes many forms, including intentionally scratching your enemy's DC Talk CD or slapping a random girl in the neck because she won't let you borrow her illustrated copy of the Children's Adventure Bible.

Pretending to speak in tongues at church camp is a pretty major sin, even if you're really good at it. Tonguing at church camp is a sin regardless of skill.

Revelation 21:8 reads: "But the cowardly, the unbelieving, the vile, the murderers, the sexually immoral, those who practice magic arts, the idolaters and all liars—they will be consigned to the fiery lake of burning sulfur." Revelation 21:9: "Except for everyone who tithed extra so Pastor Chris could build a three-car garage. Y'all are good."

Sexy Cartoon God

I stood barefoot in my grandmother's backyard, staring at the shattered gargoyle lying near the chrysanthemum bush. It was hot, July or August, the poorly tended grass prickly beneath my little corn nugget toes. I barely registered the distant clanging of an ice cream truck as I inspected the gargoyle, which had broken into a million pieces save for its leering grin. Even in death, its concrete eyes followed me. It was evil; I could see that now.

Inside, my grandmother fanned herself in the darkened living room. *"Come inside, baby girl!"* she hollered through the open window. *"Go catch that ice cream man for Nanny."* I heard her jingling through her velvet coin purse for enough quarters to buy two Tweety Bird Popsicles with gumball eyes. I took another look at the gargoyle, stuck my tongue out in a display of eight-year-old malice, and tiptoed back through the screen door.

My grandmother Susan was part Southern Baptist, part casual Pentecostal, an affiliation I suspect had more to do with her fondness for gyration than actual faith. She was an outrageous, imaginative woman, equal parts delightful, demanding, and superstitious, plying me with Popeye's Mardi Gras cheesecake as she muttered aloud to God in the living room of her cluttered rental. Her closets were full to bursting with wigs and curling irons from her days as my hometown's premier old lady hairstylist. Her bathroom, which always smelled obscenely vaginal, was littered with half-empty pill bottles and decades-old jars of Vicks VapoRub. Every single wall of her home was covered with collectibles, a haphazard gallery of framed greeting cards and wooden masks. And, of course, the gargoyle.

My grandmother acquired the gargoyle long before I was born. It was a fixture in her home, a small stone watchman hanging in the hallway outside her bedroom and guarding her king-size waterbed from evil entities. For years, the gargoyle did its job. It kept us safe as we lolled around eating Werther's caramels and gossiping about my extended family. I'm sure it saved my life a number of times; my grandmother was an enormous woman, and it's a miracle she never sleepily drifted across the waterbed's groovy tides to crush me like a log rolling down a hill. We rested easy knowing that the gargoyle kept watch—until the day my grandmother's friend Buffy came over to make salsa.

Buffy was a charismatic street preacher with a Phyllis Diller haircut and the world's tiniest glasses. She lived across the way and had inexplicably removed all the grass surrounding her home. "It is now a gravel landscape," she announced cryptically, pulling a used Kleenex out of her sleeve. Buffy is the one who taught me that God could hear your thoughts, but the Devil couldn't—unless you invited him in, either by using a Ouija board, watching sexy scenes in movies, singing the lyrics to "There's a Skeeter on My Peter (Knock It Off)," or poisoning your body with drugs and Teen Spirit deodorant.

Growing up, I'd always had some awareness of Hell. It's used as a proverbial boogeyman to keep Evangelical kids from cussing or smacking their siblings. But to Buffy, the concept was literal. She believed in an ongoing war between Good and Evil—an unending physical war, fought between invisible ectoplasmic angels and evil demons who hid under your couch and taunted your pets. If such a war exists, I'm not sure what either side is trying to achieve, although I have to imagine that the demons triumph every time a twelve-year-old boy re-uploads the BME Pain Olympics to YouTube.

Buffy believed that every sinful action, every impure thought, every bad habit strengthened Satan's army. On the day she came to make salsa, she decided that my grandmother's gargoyle was one of Satan's sneakiest soldiers. She strode through the front door, looked at the gargoyle, dropped her bag of hot peppers, and briskly declared: "Evil."

I don't know how she made that call; she visited my grandmother almost every day, so she'd seen the gargoyle plenty of times. Had the gargoyle developed a mysterious red glint in its eye overnight? Did it smell of sulfur? Maybe Buffy caught it grimacing at her footwear, a pair of men's water shoes that exposed her gnarled toenails. Didn't matter: Per Buffy, the gargoyle had to be destroyed.

My grandmother nodded her head gravely, convinced of Buffy's connection with the spiritual realm. Buffy then removed the gargoyle from the wall, placed it in the backyard, and whispered a prayer over its stony little body. I propped myself up on the kitchen counter, peering wide-eyed through the window as Buffy lifted a hammer high into the air and brought it down hard, smashing the stone gargoyle into a thousand tiny shards.

I was scared out of my mind. With a decisive swing of her hammer, Buffy confirmed my worst fear: that evil was all around us, all the time, hiding in plain sight. I left my grandmother's house lamenting my own lack of spiritual fortitude as I wondered: If that gargoyle was evil, what else was evil? Could my taped-up *NSYNC poster be trusted? Was my infant sister a harbinger of the coming apocalypse? Did my Millennium Princess Barbie house the demon Belphegor, that most gluttonous prince of Hell?

It didn't help that I already lived in a crippling state of fear. Childhood Evangelicalism is packed with ready-made rituals designed to annihilate the obsessive-compulsive brain. My brain had already begun its plunge into obsessive-compulsive territory, characterized by a series of motor tics and internal bargaining that wouldn't be properly medicated for more than a decade. I clung to my own rituals as my neuroses grew urgent and implacable, tapping doorknobs and fiddling with sink handles in an attempt to stave off the worst of my growing discomfort. Meanwhile, my faith prescribed an entirely different kind of ritual, demanding prayer, contemplation, and fealty to the dullest chapters of the New Testament.

As my obsessive tendencies blossomed, so did my desperation for order, stability, and safety. I probably would've done great in the Catholic Church, where the rules are clear. A few Hail Marys, a handful of Our Fathers, and you're good until the next transgression. Evangelicalism isn't quite as literal. I could follow the more legalistic rules of Christianity as a whole—no cussing, no kissing, no dissing—but couldn't crack the vague, spiritual stuff, including a ritual colloquially known as the Evangelical ABCs:

A: Admit that you're a sinner.

B: Believe that Jesus Christ is the literal son of God.

C: Confess your faith every chance you get.

The Evangelical church technically only asks you to complete your ABCs once, when you formally join the faith. After that, you're in. I had no problem with the first step; a lifelong goody-two-shoes, I couldn't help but admit my sinful nature to anyone who'd listen. I'd walk alongside my mom at the grocery store and rattle off my latest transgressions. "Was mean to ugly kid in music class," I listed, counting my sins on my fingers. "Lied about finishing homework." I glanced at a bulk bag of Peanut M&Ms. "Thought about stealing that just now." She'd sigh and rearrange my infant siblings in the cart, ignoring me.

I didn't mind the last step, either—the C. Like many bratty Evangelical children, I felt a sense of superiority when I confessed my faith to my less-devout peers. I'd lounge on the couch next to my friend Millie, flipping through the channels on my family's clunky circa 1999 TV remote. "Wait, stop!" Millie cried, grabbing my hand. "Go back—*Ghost Whisperer*'s on."

I rolled my eyes and pushed her hand away. "We will not be watching *Ghost Whisperer*," I explained slowly, as if addressing a simpleton. "I am a CHRIS-TI-AN."

I nailed two out of three parts of the Christian ABCs, but I waffled on the B part—the Belief. My youth pastor touted the benefit of "being pure of heart" and "walking with God," both of which were supposed to be intuitive. Neither concept made much sense to me, especially as I battled intrusive thoughts, one of the more troubling hallmarks of an OCD ramp-up. How could I be pure of heart when my brain was on twenty-four-hour taboo cinema mode? How could I walk with God if the images in my mind's eye alternated between major, *major* pervert stuff and acts of unspeakable violence? I couldn't feel secure in my salvation when some uncontrollable impulse made me picture a blank chalkboard suddenly filled with the words "God isn't real." I'd mash the heels of my hands into my eyes and try to drive the thoughts out—but the more I fought, the more powerful the thoughts became. All the while, I was convinced that I had been marked as one of Satan's own.

On average, I completed my ABCs once a month, asking God for another chance to get it exactly right. I'd kneel by the side of my bed, clasp my hands, and promise that next time would be different. Next time, I'd be able to control the intrusive thoughts. Next time, I'd resist the impulse to smack my little sister for commandeering the remote. Next time, I'd be pure of heart.

True believers will tell you that my salvation paranoia conflicts with the heart of the faith. "God loves you just as you are," they might say to soothe my fears. To that, I say: Prove it, pal. I needed rules; I needed promises. I needed a literal representation of God's love for me, preferably in the form of a solid-gold harp descending from the heavens.

I couldn't communicate these fears to anyone, especially not my parents. My mom and dad are standard-grade, no-nonsense Evangelicals. If they've ever questioned the church, they've certainly never said so. They pray every night at dinner. They vote along with the rest of the Christian Right. They listen to AM radio.

Everywhere I looked, I saw Good Christians. My grandmother watched serenely as her batshit neighbor shattered her gargoyle. My parents moved through life soothed by the surety of their own salvation. My stuck-up church friends seemed entirely without fault. Then there was me, desperately trying to shove down my confusion at the church's many contradictions.

Evangelicalism is inherently contradictory. At first, you're told that God is loving and forgiving, much chiller than the demanding punisher associated with the Baptist faith or the decadent party boy associated with Catholicism. You sing fun songs at Vacation Bible School. You wear neon T-shirts that read JESUS IS MY HOMEBOY. But Evangelicalism operates on one decidedly unchill key principle: that sinners go to Hell, and it's up to you—the seven-year-old apostle living in rural Missouri—to keep that from happening. "Picture your best friend," my youth pastor whispered earnestly, squatting on the stage in front of the children's sanctuary. "Don't you want to spend forever hanging out with them? You can—but only if they accept the word of God."

Translation: If your Jewish friend lands in Hell, that's on you. And if you fail to live up to the lofty expectations of the Evangelical church, you're gettin' sucked down the Hell Chute, too.

Same goes for any sinners in your orbit. At the time of the

gargoyle-smashing, I classified sinners as people who had doubt in their hearts, people who swore too much, people who weren't able to read their Children's Adventure Bible without getting bored, and any unfortunate soul who fails to accept the Gospel before they die. If my bejeweled denim-clad youth pastor was to be believed, the fate of these sinners was up to me. That was a problem because, as a kid, I already felt the crushing weight of the entire world on my shoulders. Now I had to shepherd the world's sinners, too? That seemed impossible, especially as I grappled with my own inadequacy as a young Christian whose brain was filled with hellish imagery.

At this point in my life, my inner monologue was one massive ongoing bargain with God. I pictured him as an omniscient version of John Smith from Disney's *Pocahontas*: sexy, blond, built like a brick shithouse, and also a cartoon. I wheeled-and-dealed with Sexy Cartoon God on a near-constant basis when faced with any crisis—and *everything* was a crisis. I'd bargain while hunkered down in the basement with my family during a tornado warning. *Hello, God?* I'd think. *If you bring my family safely through the storm, I'll bring my friend who wears Heelys roller shoes to fifth-grade worship next week.* I'd bargain as my mom drove us down the highway, promising to read three chapters of my Children's Adventure Bible if Sexy Cartoon God kept our tires from exploding as we crossed a bridge. I'd even bargain at the dinner table. *Hey, God?* I'd think, suddenly seized by one of my many irrational fears. *If you prevent this chicken fried steak from lodging in my throat and choking me to death, I will proselytize to the woman on the town square who meows like a cat.*

Sexy Cartoon God never answered back. This was concerning. "God is always speaking to us," my youth pastor would say, strutting in front of the congregation in high-priced leather flip-flops. "You just have to open your heart and surrender." *Well, my fine fellow, that's too bad,* I'd think. *I'm physically incapable of surrendering.*

In Evangelicalism, the concept of surrender is sacrosanct. There are songs, texts, and prayer templates all dedicated to the idea of surrendering to God's will. Believers must surrender their egos, their plans, their personal desires and impulses, with the understanding that Father Knows Best. To surrender is to pursue peace, to achieve the kind of serenity that comes when someone else takes the steering wheel. None of these words meant anything to me. Without reviewing a literal scroll of God's to-the-minute demands, I had no idea what was being asked of me.

Lack of faith aside, my inability to surrender should've been a clue as to the dawning of my glamorous neurological disorder. At the time, though, I assumed it was some sort of curse, as though I alone bore a sacred duty to keep the world turning through a complex series of rituals and tics. I was sure that my sheer will—along with my habit of tapping the church doorknob five times upon entering and exiting—was the only thing standing between my youth group and deadly spontaneous combustion. This wasn't my only ritual; before I could drift off to sleep, I had to draw eight invisible circles above my bed with my pointer finger. I convinced myself that, if I failed to move my feet correctly while walking, someone in my family would die. The closest I got to surrender was gliding at a marginally high speed at the roller-skating rink.

When Evangelicals ask you to surrender, they also present you with a robust list of things to be afraid of. How can you surrender to Christ's serenity when evil lurks around every corner, taking the shape of something as innocuous as a stone gargoyle? How are you supposed to walk calmly with God knowing that Satan's shiny red ass is conjuring up all sorts of smutty movies, secular music, and other fripperies meant to activate your genitals and open your soul up to evil? I couldn't surrender, nor could I enjoy myself. There was only one thing to do: fake it till I made it. I had to perform Evangelical Excellence.

My pursuit of Evangelical Excellence peaked in the summers.

During the month of June, I'd cram my feet into a pair of Tevas and haul my duffel bag to church camp. There I swatted mosquitos, screamed the words to John 3:16, and peered hornily at Christian boys during the annual Kamp Hoedown. I even braved the Blob, the marine attraction that achieved commercial recognition in the 1995 film *Heavyweights*. The Blob was a giant canvas pillow accessible only by leaping off a fifteen-foot platform, the perfect metaphor for Christlike surrender. I leapt off the platform and missed the Blob entirely, landing in the water with a *thwack*, torso aflame with the sting of ten thousand belly flops. Another failed surrender; another epic swan dive into the churning waters of spiritual failure. (Years later, the camp came under scrutiny after evidence emerged of ongoing sexual abuse by a male camp counselor. Today, the camp's website features a page titled "Our Response to Abuse and Child Safety." The web page header image is, incredibly, a photo of the Blob.)

Me at church camp, clearly already damned.

Church camp was the best place to perform Evangelical Excellence. We'd pile into the echoey gym and weep as good-looking worship band members strummed an hour's worth of nonstop, high-octane, intensely emotional interludes. These sessions were a lot like your standard rock concert, though instead of worshipping at the altar of shredding the ax, we worshipped at the altar of capitalistic Christianity. "You're gonna see that collection plate coming around," crooned the worship band's handsome bassist, Dan. "This is your chance to give back to your community if you feel the Spirit move you." By "give back," he meant "chuck your meager allowance into the collection plate to help fund a new pyrotechnic display for the camp's Fourth of July Worship-Thon." If it wasn't the Worship-Thon, it was a flashy new tour bus for the church band, a raise for the head pastor, or the promise of clean water for an emaciated child named Lovely in some remote land that hadn't yet been touched by the splendor of white Jesus.

There is no savvier grift than passing the collection plate while the summer camp praise band plays. I gave every time. Once, I dumped my entire weekly camp allowance—twenty or thirty bucks—into the collection plate, convinced that the Spirit was speaking to me. Turns out it was just a series of powerful minor chords. (Shortly after, the band's babysitter/beautiful lead singer shared some home truths. When she paused her rendition of "Our God (Is an Awesome God)," she rubbed her pregnant belly and looked out peacefully from the makeshift stage. "Remember, you guys," she crooned. "If you're having premarital sex, you're sullying someone else's future husband or wife." I raised my hands heavenward and nodded.)

The most important measure of Evangelical Excellence involved the camp's motto: "God First, Others Second, Me Third." At the end of each session, one camper was awarded the Me Third award, given to the kid who showed the strongest display of selflessness. More often than not, the honor went to an incredibly bitchy girl who manhandled other campers in an attempt to position herself at the very back of the breakfast line. She'd smile sweetly as the counselors passed, nodding approvingly at her selfless display. Later that day, the bitchy girl shoved a skinny girl into the mud on the kickball field. She waited a moment until the camp photographer passed by, then extended her hand to haul her teammate back to her feet, smiling for the camera.

If you profess that God comes first in all things, it stands to reason that every aspect of your life—your achievements, your talents, even your earthly possessions—must exist to further the Kingdom of God. God's children can get away with pretty much anything as long as they say, loudly, that their actions are for the glory of the Lord. I think of Tim Tebow, whose net worth currently sits at a cozy $71 million, ripping across the end zone and collecting checks. I think of the frontwoman of the praise band clearly writhing with pleasure at the opportunity to rip her stellar high C in front of a crowd of five hundred. More than anything, I think of prosperity gospel: the uniquely Evangelical idea that God wants you to revel in obscene wealth and abundance—all for the glory of God.

Prosperity gospel drives home the Evangelical church's most harmful lesson: that the Lord rewards those who live by his word, and He rewards them *handsomely*. Modern Evangelicals tend to interpret this in the most material way possible. A labyrinthine house, a sick whip, a flashy pair of designer jeans—all proof that you're doing the Lord's work. The poor, on the other hand? They're clearly not in with the big guy upstairs. It establishes a sense of superiority among wealthy Evangelicals, allowing them to justify nearly any action as one of God's chosen few. Sure, you can pray for the poor. You can even throw on matching T-shirts and volunteer among them for a few hours once a year—as long as you remember that, at the end of the day, *you're* the righteous one.

I saw this firsthand when I leveled up from church camp and embarked on a series of mission trips to Nicaragua. At fifteen, mission trips were the best. Take a trip to Central America with no real skills and no understanding of the political intricacies of the region?

Leech off a culture to feel better about myself? Receive a standing ovation in the main service—not the youth service, the *main* service—for furthering the kingdom of Heaven? Post a Facebook photo album titled "They Taught Me More Than I Taught Them"? Delicious, delicious—until I realized that mission trips are bad news, a revelation I had after seeing one too many wealthy white women with huge fake boobs, intense fake tans, and enormous diamond wedding rings posing next to gaggles of skinny Nicaraguan children and giggling, "Yo-la!"

About this time, my Evangelical anxiety reached critical mass. I couldn't stomach another mission trip; I could barely pay attention in church without slipping into a frenzy of motor tics. I began to feel uncomfortable around my church friends, who were either genuinely more righteous than me or just better at pretending. They never expressed doubts or lustful thoughts. They fell asleep early at youth group lock-ins, snoring gently as I lay awake, fretting over the state of my mortal soul. They had clear skin, a definite sign that they were God's faves.

They also carried themselves with a sort of grace that I never managed to cultivate. They never cussed—never even seemed *tempted* to cuss, even after losing at Dance Dance Revolution. They never got in trouble for shooting their Communion grape juice like Sam Elliott in *Road House*. They never rifled through the prayer request bucket in search of juicy gossip. They never scanned the crowd at the annual church retreat in search of the hottest piece of Christian ass. They had this *serenity* that I couldn't seem to muster. In hindsight, I was just a hyperactive loudmouth. That's not an indictment of my Heavenly value—but at the time, I felt like garbage among these self-assured teens who seemed perfectly happy to walk with the Lord.

I suppose I could've voiced my fears, but I couldn't bring myself to confess. Mostly because I worried that my church friends would find me unworthy and stop inviting me to sleepovers. More than that, I believed Buffy's message: that evil was all around us, all the time, just waiting to prey on our vulnerabilities. If I spoke my fears aloud, the *Devil might hear.* There was no telling what he'd do with the information.

"Satan's army will use your fear to draw you further from the Light," Buffy had explained, dusting bits of gargoyle off her jeans. I wasn't sure what this meant, but I was pretty confident that Satan was just waiting for the right moment to exploit, say, my fear of dying in a fiery plane crash, or choking on a Dorito, or waking up to find that my parents had moved away without telling me. I pictured a victorious Satan crooning to me in a deep baritone. "Sorry, baby," he'd say, filing his pointy black stiletto nails with one of Hitler's incisors. "It was just too fun to pass up."

Instead of owning up to my doubts, I doubled down. I tried to convert my school friends to Evangelicalism like they were prizes to be won. I asked my parents for a purity ring for my sixteenth birthday. I attempted to minister to the woman on the town square who meowed like a cat. She stared at me, opened her mouth wide, and screamed: "WHORE!"

I spent my entire adolescence trying to feel close to God. Nothing worked. My neurological concerns ensured that my entire existence was already dictated by fear; fear-based Evangelical teachings made that worse. Not only did I fear failing at one of my many rituals; I feared that I was too stupid to understand my church's obscure teachings, that I was destined for Hades because I was too anxious to trust in the Lord, and that I'd never hear God speaking to me because my head was already full of noise. Worst of all, I feared the invisible evil that circled me, hyena-like, whether it be in the form of a tiny stone gargoyle or my own inadequacy.

Evangelicalism is built on internal dread, fueled by parishioners' most intimate insecurities. In acknowledging that all have sinned and fall short of the glory of God, Evangelicalism asks: What if you fail to convert the rest of the world's population? What if you're not pure of heart? What if you're not walking with God 24/7? *What if you're not good enough?*

Eventually, there was nothing left to do but shrug. I realized I'd probably never perform inner peace the way my church friends did. I acknowledged that I'd probably never be a good Christian. I tiptoed away from the sanctuary, went home, and started adjusting to a life without constant fear of fire and brimstone.

It's been about a decade since I left the church, spurred largely by the icky feeling after my last mission trip. Leaving the church coincided with my political awakening, when I realized that my leftism didn't quite square with the prosperity doctrine of Missouri Evangelicals. And while some former Evangelicals have stories of storming out, leaving the church in a moment of satisfying ire, my leaving was less decisive than that. I'd like to say that I pulled a Ferris Bueller–style getaway, slamming the door of my Nissan Maxima and speeding away in style, blaring my novelty La Cucaracha horn all the way home. In reality, my departure was more of a sputtering exit.

Twice, I crept back to the church. The first time was after a few dates with a curly-haired Christian boy who took me on a moonlit hike, got very close to my face, and told me we had to part ways because he needed to focus on his relationship with God. In hindsight, that should've been enough to send me punting my old Children's Adventure Bible across the interstate. Unfortunately, at the time, my immediate reaction was to briefly contort myself into the shape of a good Evangelical in an attempt to win him back. A few weeks later, I saw him at a bar with a much hotter girl. Spell broken.

The second time, I let myself get roped into a Bible study for college girls. I was bored and lonely, dissatisfied with my mean college friends. I can't blame myself for being absorbed into the Bible study's orbit—they had donuts and sweet smiles and called me "girlfriend" in a way that reminded me of my old camp counselors. I stuck it out for a few months, relearning all the old Evangelical buzzwords in a final attempt at true belief. We walked in faith. We *did life together*. We *laid hands* on each other to pray. We confessed what lay *on our hearts*. It didn't work. They were nice girls, but I still felt like a pretender. The group disbanded after a few months, sending me back into secularism. Last I checked, the leader of the group had turned to witchcraft, selling spells and sex oils on Instagram. I'm happy for her.

There's nothing remarkable about my experience hauling myself out of the Evangelical trenches. I was luckier than some, able to find a strong community outside of church in relatively little time. Still, it's weird. To this day, my mom passive-aggressively asks me to say grace at the dinner table. She'll close her eyes, bow her head, and wait, opening one eye to peer at me, snakelike. "Oh, I forgot," she'll say. "You don't *pray* anymore."

I'd be lying if I said I didn't miss some aspects of the routine: hauling myself out of bed on Sunday mornings and sipping coffee on padded folding chairs while familiar worship songs blare around me. I don't have to believe in the Gospel to miss high-fiving the ushers, some of whom I'd known since I was two. And it goes without saying that I miss the peculiar delight of Church Lunch, that ritualistic trip to Rib Crib for a platter of post-service chicken fingers. Nothing like absorbing the Lord's teachings while cramming onion rings down your righteous gullet.

I'm a creature of routine, and I still feel a bit adrift without the weekly marker that is the Sunday morning early service. I'm trying to forgive myself for feeling the urge to perform some kind of ritual when my neighborhood church bells ring. Maybe *ritual* is the wrong word—outside of grape juice Communion, the only real rite in Evangelicalism is trying to get your hair bigger and bigger. I guess what I'm feeling is the impulse to pray.

At this point, I'm not even sure who I'd pray to. I can't pray to the Evangelical god, because He still casts wives as subservient to their husbands and convinced teenage me that I was destined to rot in Hell. I can't pray to the Catholic god, lest I anger my radical Huguenot ancestors who slipped out of France in ramshackle boats blaring "We're Not Gonna Take It" over primitive loudspeakers. So instead, I continue to flagellate myself at some obscure altar entirely based in paranoia. I ditched the church, but I kept the fear. I've lost the fear of Hell, but I have plenty of other irrational fears. I worry that a stray Rollerblader will annihilate my beagle. I worry that my brother will drink too much and fall into the lake. I worry that the citizens of WhoVille were too mean to the Grinch. Better than fearing eternal damnation, I guess.

My only consolation is that I'm finally old enough to purchase a gargoyle-smashing hammer of my very own. Maybe that's what I'm doing right now. With every joke I write, maybe I'm chipping away at the fear I was raised on. For a long time, I thought it protected me. Now, I feel ready to take that fear into my backyard. I'll smash it with a hammer until it's unrecognizable. Then I'll brush the shards off my jeans and walk away, leaving the gargoyle to leer lazily at the chrysanthemum bushes. If Sexy Cartoon God's got a problem with that, He'll need to be a bit more clear.

Tiny Dainty
Baby Lady

I f you attended public school between the years 1957 and 2013, you know the infernal scourge that was the Presidential Fitness Test. The test was issued twice a year by gym teachers across the country, involving a series of exercises that ranged from the bizarre (the arm hang, useful only in an international spy scenario and/or sinkhole disaster) to the humiliating (the Progressive Aerobic Cardiovascular Endurance Run, or PACER, also known as a Shuttle Run, during which the unfortunate child must run back and forth until they collapse from exhaustion).

The Presidential Fitness Test emerged in the late 1950s to chisel American youths into lean, mean, fighting machines. This isn't hyperbole; there's strong evidence that the test was designed during the Eisenhower years to cultivate military excellence in kids barely old enough to button their pants. Still, the test lingered long after the Cold War, masquerading as a means to assess the baseline fitness level of American schoolchildren. In reality, it was a mechanism to weed out the weenies. In the early 2000s, more than thirty years after Eisenhower's death, the Presidential Fitness Test was still propelling hot jocks to gym class glory. And I was anything but a hot jock.

The Presidential Fitness Test was my Gehenna, condensing all the things I hated about gym class into one weeklong tribulation. I had terrible asthma and dissolved into wheezing fits after a few jumping jacks. I was also uncoordinated, as evidenced by my catastrophic stint on a YMCA peewee soccer team. I don't remember much about that season, other than the leering presence of my teammate Dallas, who was a biter. My dad remembers everything, including the day I scored my only goal. "The ball bounced off of your head and into the other team's goal," he claims, guffawing at the dinner table. "We bought you a Barbie to celebrate."

After that, I veered away from activities that involved rapid movement of any kind. That's partially because I was a tall, beefy kid and felt horribly conspicuous even while standing still. Today, I teeter on the edge of five foot six, which is tall enough to caddy for a Victoria's Secret model but not so tall that I can hang string lights on my patio unassisted. Five foot six is a perfectly middling height. The problem is that I've been this height since I was ten.

At five foot six, I loomed over the hot jock boys in my fifth-grade class. This was a nightmare. While there's now plenty of messaging surrounding the inherent sexiness of big, bold, tall women, we can all agree that there's something off-putting about the act of looming—especially when the loomer is a fifth-grade girl who barreled past gap-toothed cuteness and landed in the husky end of the ninety-fifth height percentile. Even before I reached my full height, I radiated oafishness. Once, I jumped so hard on my friend's twin bed that the frame quite literally shattered beneath me. Another time, I accidentally tore the nozzle off a Jacuzzi tub jet. The jet wasn't powerful enough for my liking, so I reached over and gave it a good crank. The nozzle fell into one of my gigantic child hands, and gallons of water rained destruction on the bathroom as I ran nude down the hallway screaming, "FLOOD! FLOOD!!!!"

I made a few early attempts to muster poise. After the Jacuzzi incident, my parents chucked me into ballet class. There I learned to slick my hair greasies back into a tight bun and point my toes alongside blue-eyed girls with tidy elfin features. I had no elfin features; I was all chubby cheeks and dimpled knees, a fleshy, pink assortment of circles. I stuck it out long enough to get a bit role in the studio's annual production of *The Nutcracker*. The day of the performance, my mom crammed my tater-tot body into pale pink tights and a matching leotard, mashed some whorish Cyndi Lauper lipstick across my toothy grin, and left me at the stage door. Two hours later, my parents picked me up with a bouquet of roses and a reel of camcorder video footage that clearly showed me wrenching my leotard out of my butt midway through the Dance of the Sugar Plum Fairy. They shook their heads sadly. Ballerinas don't pick wedgies.

Me enjoying the art of dance.

A few years later, I saw a martial arts demonstration at church. A woman with a thick braid padded onstage in a crisp white taekwondo uniform, followed by a hairy, muscular man whose pants were stretched obscenely across his huge man ass. I remember the

ass clearly, because it was the first time I had seen buttocks so muscular, so delightfully protruding, so capable of pulling pants taut so
the seat formed a tight bridge betwixt the cheeks. I tore my eyes
away from the stupendous ass just in time to see the uniformed pair
rip a synchronized flying side kick, simultaneously screaming, "THE
HANDS AND FEET OF CHRIST ARE MIGHTY AND SWIFT!"

Later that day, I threw a huge fit and demanded that my parents
enroll me in taekwondo classes. I jumped on my bed and tried to
punch the ceiling fan, excitedly shouting my intention to become
mighty and swift! I was excited to find my place among the lithe,
powerful athletes in southwest Missouri's martial arts scene. After
a few sessions in the armpit-smelling dojang, I realized that lithe,
powerful athletes are few and far between in southwest Missouri's
martial arts scene, although there are more than a few Caucasian
break dancers in the mix.

Time and time again, I failed to cultivate any sort of athletic
grace. I couldn't score a soccer goal to save my life. I was the shame
of the local ballet school. I hated my scratchy taekwondo uniform. I
was unsure of my body and unable to force my strange, unknowable
muscles into the sort of athleticism that could make me worthy of a
Livestrong bracelet. Instead, I *loomed*.

I failed to loom productively—that is, to loom in a way that
could earn my gym teacher's favor and score me a spot in the Evangelical girls' basketball league. No, my looming was *Munsters*-esque.
While my friends were shimmying across the monkey bars in their
dELiA*s pedal pushers, I was navigating the aisles of Kohl's alone,
trying to disguise my prepubescent bulk under layers of Happy
Bunny T-shirts and zip-off cargo pants. I felt huge and clunky and
hideous and weird, neither tall, thin, and stately, nor short, perky,
and cute as a button. There's simply no playbook for unathletic girls
who find themselves destroying Jacuzzi tubs and *looming*.

The Presidential Fitness Test underscored my oafish tendencies. The pull-up test sent me tumbling to the ground, all floppy

limbs and too-tight cotton gym shorts. The sit-up test was a fart bomb waiting to happen. The PACER left me traumatized; even now, I can hear the recording, narrated by a chipper southern woman who sounded like a cross between a Stepford Wife and the meanest TJ Maxx manager you can possibly imagine. "The PACER will begin in thirty seconds," the narrator twanged. "Line up at the start." At that point, we'd line up at one end of the school gym and wait for the prerecorded bell that would prompt us to sprint to the other end.

"The running speed starts slowly, but gets faster each minute," explained the narrator in a righteous drawl typically only employed by hosts of ladies' Bible studies who want to make it clear that store-bought chicken salad will not be tolerated. Then, the stampede. *DING* went the bell, *SWISH* went my classmates' shorts as they scrambled to make it to the other side of the gym before the next bell clanged. *WHUMP* went my bod as I tripped over my Sketchers and slunk to the sidelines, defeated after only a few *DINGs*.

Even worse was the mile run, which exacerbated my asthma in a pathetically public capacity. On one occasion, I stumbled through the first quarter of the race, shoulders heaving, then dragged myself off the track to plead with my gym teacher. He was a tall, spindly man in track pants, with wire-framed glasses that accentuated his beady eyes. "Coach Green, I can't breathe," I gasped, gesturing wildly toward the nurse's office. He stared down at me, sternly toying with the whistle hanging around his neck. "*Inhaler, inhaler!!!*" I croaked, scratching at my throat. He clicked his pen and made a discreet note on his clipboard.

"All right," he replied, looking at me like I had sneezed on his Reeboks. "But I'm putting you down as a seventeen-minute miler."

A seventeen-minute miler. It was more than a grade; it was a permanent classification. I had been born a seventeen-minute-miler, and I'd die a seventeen-minute-miler, the way some people were born with blue eyes and some with green. You either had it or you didn't, and I most certainly didn't. In hindsight, it's not like I was particularly prepared for the Presidential Fitness Test. There was no Couch-to-5K program for looming fifth graders; our class curriculum was mostly limited to playing parachute while Coach Green showered praise on his sporty faves. No attention was paid to the seventeen-minute milers, a group that included me and Edgar, a tiny goth who wore huge T-shirts and taught me to play dirty M.A.S.H.

Relegated to the seventeen-minute-mile club, I fell further and further behind my speedy peers. "Sports aren't for me," I'd warn my junior high gym classmates during mandatory team sports units. I used it as a sort of disclaimer: Sports *aren't for me*, so you can't blame me when I accidentally send the kickball flying into the direct center of your crotch. Sports *aren't for me,* so it won't hurt my feelings when our leathery gym teacher mistakes me for a girl who graduated seven years ago. Anyway, there were more important things to worry about, like slipping a note into Ian Porter's locker to ask if he'd like to go out for an appropriately supervised linguine date sometime.

I certainly didn't feel great about my lack of athleticism; it's more that I was resigned to the fact that I'd never know the joy of working up a mean, frothy sweat. Sure, I made the occasional spirited attempt to find my sport. Halfway through my freshman year of high school, my best friend paused my MP3 player—I was writhing in pleasure as the new Fall Out Boy album destroyed my teenage eardrums—and made an announcement. "I'm going out for the soccer team," she proclaimed, steeling herself for my reaction.

I chewed over the implications. On one hand, I couldn't run more than half a mile, had no idea how to kick a ball, and had barely processed the trauma of my martial arts career. On the other, I wasn't about to lose my friend to the hot jocks. I had also just been left off the cast list for our school's spring production of *Fame*, and I really wanted attention. I pictured my friend and I sprinting down the field, passing the ball between our tan, muscled bodies, scoring a goal as the drama teacher looked on. "Damn," she'd say. "I really should've cast Lillian in *Fame*."

The next day, I found myself plodding down the soccer field, secondhand cleats full of Astroturf. It was five years after the seventeen-minute-mile incident with Coach Green, but it's not like I spent those years learning how to increase my cardiovascular endurance. I was right back where I started: hauling myself off the track to beg for the coach's mercy. "Coach, I need a break," I gasped, gesturing wildly toward the bench. She looked at me sideways, distractedly picking turf out of her lady mullet. Like Coach Green, she clicked her pen and made a note on her clipboard. Two days later, I was off the team.

I made a few more halfhearted attempts to find my sport. I doggy-paddled my way through an entire season on the high school swim team, mostly because the sport didn't garner enough interest for the coach to make cuts. Prior to that experience, my swimming career was purely recreational. I spent most summer days at our shabby neighborhood pool, but I had never learned the art of the freestyle stroke. I was too busy squatting in the shallow end, lowering myself until the water came up to my cheekbones. This allowed me to discreetly stare at the hot lifeguard, eyes shifting to and fro, like an alligator in a swamp.

While I did learn the basics of competitive swimming, I never advanced past the slow lane. Our coach didn't have time to train up a new swimmer, especially one without any sort of competitive potential. Instead she left me and a few other hopeless recruits to our own devices. Largely unsupervised, we snapped our racing suit straps to the tune of the National Anthem and held obscene underwater photo shoots with the equipment manager's waterproof camera. We did work out alongside the rest of the team, holding planks and pumping iron and frantically paddling from one end of the pool to the other. Along the way, something strange happened: Somehow, in between lazy backflips, my body started to change. For the first time in my life, I had visible tricep definition. I gained muscle but lost a dress size or two. I couldn't see it at the time, but the difference was stark.

Around that time, people started commenting on my body. A classmate remarked at how quickly I had shed my lingering baby fat after a few months on the swim team. At Thanksgiving, my uncle looked me up and down and proclaimed, "Lillian, you get prettier and skinnier every time I see you," as if the two were inextricably linked. For the first time in my life, I was lauded for leanness. The comments grew into a cacophony of voices, all telling me the same thing: *Hey, baby, let's get skinnier.*

I, like everyone else, grew up flooded with messages that paint smallness as goodness. The messages started early, transmitted by willowy Disney heroines and literary heroines like *Little House on the Prairie*'s Ma Wilder. The latter was described as having feet half the size of Pa Wilder's and a waist you could easily circle with two hands. *Everybody* wanted to fuck Ma Wilder.

Later, my peers and I took our body image cues from *Us Weekly*, a publication packed with clippings of skeletal starlets. We'd stare at Nicole Richie's birdlike frame, circling our wrists with thumb and middle finger to determine if we were "big-boned." By that standard, I wasn't just big-boned—I might as well have been the secret spawn of an unmarried giantess who dropped me on my parents' doorstep so she could get back to skanking around.

Meanwhile, the older women in my life welcomed me into the shadowy realm of three-day celery cleanses and fluorescent-lit Weight Watchers meetings. It wasn't anything they said; unlike some of my peers' WASPy moms, mine never urged me to join her in diet purgatory. It was more like a rite of passage, a silent salute as I slipped into the Splenda-scented waters of body-conscious adolescence. I'd mention calories in passing and watch my female relatives exhale with a combination of relief and resignation. Looking back, I picture them as weary souls swirling about in the River Styx. "Greetings," they'd sigh as I dipped a toe into the chilly depths.

"We've been expecting you."

The urgent pursuit of thinness felt inescapable, especially given the messaging of the mid-2000s and early 2010s. At that point, the flagrant eating disorders of the early aughts were out of fashion; they had been disguised and repackaged as clean eating, sold alongside diet pills that made consumers physically leak out excess dietary fat. The stars were still rail-thin, but no one talked about dieting. Thinness was supposed to seem effortless, though everyone knew it wasn't. And so I teetered into womanhood, trying to find the perfect balance between projecting confidence and discussing my own self-hatred with the women in my life to seem more like an adult. I don't blame them. They slipped into womanhood the same way I did: by trying to squeeze through a progressively shrinking Ma Wilder–shaped hole in the wall.

Back then, there was a distinct lack of wistful chatter surrounding women like me. Average-sized women with thick calves and camp counselor vibes are great at making macramé key chains, but no way were we voluptuous enough to inspire the dirty ditties of the mid-aughts. This was the era of Mariah Carey's "Touch My Body" and Ludacris's "Money Maker" and Lady Gaga's "Beautiful Dirty Rich." To be ditty-worthy, you're either packing major titty meat or you're long, lithe, and catlike. I have always been somewhere in the middle—but when people started commenting on my post-swim-season body, I felt as though the tides were starting to turn. In my little raisin brain, athleticism automatically resulted in thinness. And like I mentioned earlier, thinness was goodness. If we look to the transitive property, we can make the following conclusion: Athleticism results in thinness, and thinness is goodness; ergo, athleticism is goodness. I wasn't a natural athlete, and I certainly wouldn't be invited back to the swim team. But people around me seemed pleased when I debuted my thinner body. With that, I reasoned: If I became very, *very* thin, I could retain some semblance of social capital. Organized sports were out of the question, so I had to get creative. I turned to the premier sport for clumsy girls who hate themselves: running.

After the seventeen-minute mile, I did everything I could to avoid running. I had no interest in plodding around a black asphalt track; I observed my school's cross-country team with suspicion. "Freaks, all of 'em," I'd declare, sitting in my nondescript sedan as the skeletal boys' team warmed up in the school parking lot, their knees clacking together like a herd of newborn colts. Once, I pulled into the lot just as the runners returned from a distance jog. I laid on my horn, a novelty La Cucaracha tooter that I'd had installed for my seventeenth birthday. It wailed—*BEH DEH DEH DEH DEHHHH*—and startled the poorly insulated athletes as they completed their final meter. I drove by slowly, lowering my window Cruella de Vil–style and shaking my head at the sheer lunacy of running on purpose.

My attitude shifted when I left the swim team in disgrace. I was terrified of putting on a single pound, afraid to lose the approval of those around me who, for whatever reason, concerned themselves with the precise protrusion of my collarbones. It was then that I read about the power of daily jogging in *Seventeen* magazine—"The perfect way to get lean and toned for bikini season."

Lean and Toned. LEAN *AND* TONED. Per *Seventeen*, all I had to do was run a mile a day and I would not be simply Lean, but also Toned. *Seventeen* made no mention of stress relief, functional endurance, or the joy of movement. Running was painted strictly as a skinny-inducing mechanism, which intrigued me immediately. Unfortunately, the task itself seemed impossible.

It wasn't just that I had never run a mile; it was that I genuinely had no idea *how* to run a mile. I simply was not equipped. I owned one sports bra, an impossibly tight Pepto-Bismol pink number I bought for my failed soccer tryout. My asthmatic lungs were weak, and I was so out of touch with my limbs that I could barely tell the difference between everyday soreness and a shattered tibia. My body was foreign to me, a vessel for embarrassment and betrayal and occasional weird boob stuff with the spiky-haired boy down the street. The only thing spurring me on was an MP3 player packed with filthy Ashlee Simpson tracks. This is how I, the least-prepared person on the planet, went out for my first jog.

A few steps in, I felt a twinge in my ankle. A few more steps, and my sports bra started to chafe. My earbuds kept falling out. I didn't know if I should land on my toes or my heel, so I alternated, improvising a gait that made me look like a haunted marionette doll. "Pretend you're holding potato chips between your thumb and forefinger while you run," one of my sporty friends had advised earlier that day. "It'll distract you until you find your pace." It didn't distract me, but it did leave me hurtling down the street with both hands thrust forward forming "Okay" signs. "OKAY," I yelled to no one. "OKAY!!!!!!!!!"

Still, the lure of being skinny was greater than my own comfort. I craved more approving glances from relatives and enjoyed the special attention paid by the grocery bagger at the Price Cutter up the road. My failed stint on the swim team gave me a close look into the benefits of shrinking myself. These were also peak *Biggest Loser* years, a program that helped internalize the idea that physical fitness had to be the result of stunning discomfort. With that, I dedicated myself to daily misery.

I managed to slap on a bit more mileage during my teen years, working up to running for twenty whole minutes at a time. I used neighbors' houses as my goalposts, promising myself that I'd make it to the blue house at the end of the street one day, then to the yellow house around the corner the next, and finally to the run-down bungalow with an army of stone geese dotting the overgrown lawn. If you enjoy running, this is a fine technique for building endurance. But I didn't enjoy a second of it. Every mile I logged was pure torture, propelled only by the desire to shed what little body fat I had. There wasn't much to shed; I was thinner than I'd ever been, with collarbones that poked through my high-necked tees. But I still felt oafish and awkward, caught up in the self-hatred that blooms once you realize there's no such thing as small enough.

By the time I hobbled unsteadily into college, my relationship with my body was so confusing that I began to doubt the reality of my own perfectly average flesh. I had gained back a bit of my swimming weight but was still objectively tiny, parading around in a size four. Still, I could stand next to a person my exact shape and size and feel horribly conspicuous, like I was towering over them in a way that attracted the worst sort of attention. I wasn't sure what my body actually looked like, though I was positive that a single uncounted calorie would send me spiraling into a pit of chaos. I slept in late to avoid eating breakfast or lunch. I drank cheap vodka mixed with raspberry lemonade Crystal Light in lieu of high-calorie beer. Surrounded by booze and idiots, I let fad diets and self-imposed starvation wash over me like waves over a low-carb, cottage cheese–ridden shore. All because I simply couldn't think of anything worse than being . . . what, *large?*

The problem with fad diets is they all have different rules, and I'm a sucker for rules. Weight Watchers employs a complex point system, while the Five-Bite Diet only allows practitioners to take five bites at any given meal. But my personal favorites were the diets that banned entire food groups, like Atkins and the Paleo diet. These diets forbid sugar, bread, and other complex carbs, leaving the dieter to subsist mostly on meat and eggs. I even courted the egg-fast community, a group of oily acolytes who eat nothing but eggs, butter, and cheese for three days at a time in an effort to facilitate rapid weight loss. During my egg fast, I blasted my roommate with ungodly flatulence and left countless yolk-coated skillets to "soak" in the sink. I lost four pounds of water weight, gained them all back the following weekend, and developed a lifelong aversion to eggs. That summer, I switched from eggs to laxative teas and devoted myself to running sprints with a classmate. "We're gonna get so skinny," she panted, hunched over on the sidewalk after another underfed cardio session. "Yeah, for sure," I agreed, stirring my laxative tea with the enthusiasm of someone who tortures herself to remain palatable for fraternity members in bad suits. "So skinny."

In Norway, athletic institutions are governed by a doctrine known as Children's Rights in Sport. Introduced in 1987, the document dictates the conditions under which Norwegian children may engage in athletic pursuits, all in pursuit of a singular vision: promoting "Joy of Sport for All." Kids get to choose whether or not they'd like to participate in competitions, and they aren't often placed on rigorous traveling teams. The conditions are strict, with hefty fines for sports organizations that break the rules. As the National Olympic Committee of Norway puts it, "children should have a social environment around sports, feel safe, want to try new things and not be afraid to make mistakes."

Growing up, I most definitely did not feel safe around sports. I had been tidily sorted into the seventeen-minute-mile club at age ten and left to languish without any sort of athletic tutelage. My approach to fitness was entirely rooted in terror: first, the terror of trying something new and garnering the disdain of those around me; later, the terror of losing what control I thought I had over my body. Either way, it felt safer to declare that sports *weren't for me*. That way, I could isolate myself entirely from the athletic realm, turning instead to punishing forms of movement in hopes that something—anything—would deliver the Lean and Toned (LEAN! AND! TONED!!!!!!) physique promised in *Seventeen* magazine.

By the time I reached my mid-twenties, I felt chronically disconnected from my body. My corporeal form felt like a collection of mismatched Tinker Toys, operating in ways both mysterious and disgusting. My running habit became frenzied as I sought the pace that would finally whittle my physical form away into nothingness. I choked down Lean Cuisines and weighed myself multiple times a day, looking for ways to reduce my daily water weight fluctuations with the commitment of a mad scientist. I could be mean, I could be malnourished—but, my God, I could not simply be *large*.

Meanwhile, I disregarded the ways I actually *liked* to move. In my head, I was a lazy lump of a woman. In reality, I spent my weekends scrabbling up rocky hiking trails. I gyrated to Robyn until my beagle howled in protest. I took fitness classes that involved pounding giant tires with sledgehammers, which made me feel like a Viking in the best way. But even though these activities all fell under the umbrella of fitness, I still associated working out with misery. Thus, I reasoned, any sort of enjoyable physical activity probably wouldn't produce the results I was looking for. I could scrabble up all the trails I wanted; it didn't make me an *athlete* worthy of *fuel* or *respect*. Pounding a tire with a sledgehammer had no value unless it contributed to my ultimate goal: disappearing, one calorie at a time.

For all my self-imposed bodily torture, I felt no more capable of carrying my twenty-five-pound dog up four flights of stairs to my apartment. I hadn't achieved Jillian Michaels shoulders despite eating 1,450 calories a day and screaming into my pillow on the days when I surpassed that calorie limit. I wasn't Lean or Toned; I certainly wasn't strong. I also wasn't sleeping, partially because I wasn't eating nearly enough food, but also because I dreaded my morning high-intensity interval workouts with an impassioned anxiety that kept me awake for hours. Knowing I'd have to wake up at 6 a.m. so a large, handsome Nordic man could frown at me as I fumbled with a rowing machine gave me round-the-clock nausea, even as I professed that I'd never felt better.

This is how I found myself creeping Gollum-like into a weight room. A particularly brutal cycle of self-loathing had left my skin broken out and scabby, my hair and nails brittle and broken. I needed a new approach. Mysteriously, my Instagram feed had become filled with female powerlifters completing impossible feats of strength and eating enormous portions of oats. These women were unlike any I had ever seen. They had rippling biceps and broad smiles. They didn't look like they were even a little starving. They were absolutely capable of surviving the apocalypse, a concern that I've always kept top of mind. Even stranger, they weren't doing any of the activities I had come to associate with an acceptable performance of fitness. There were no PACER tests. There were no arduous miles being logged—only triumphant, well-fueled miles. There was no talk of whittling away at oneself. These women were lifting heavy things above their heads, and they all had one goal: to get bigger, not smaller. Bigger in the physical sense, yes; some of these broads had shoulders that could support a pair of oxen, no question. But also bigger in the philosophical sense. They wanted to be stronger, louder, faster, and more audacious than their leotard-sporting, aerobics-instructing forebears. They wanted *more*.

I wanted more, too. I canceled my obscenely expensive gym membership and switched to a rock-climbing gym with a no-frills weight room full of hard metal objects. I took a one-on-one introductory bouldering class, during which the instructor told me I had "good fall instincts." I took this as a nice way of saying "you'll be falling a lot, but your natural instinct to curl up into a ball will serve you well." I then hauled myself into the weight room for the first time, armed with a little pink lifting notebook I had purchased for the occasion. I had filled it out the night before, writing out my lifts in bubble letters like an excited fourth grader going back to school. I visualized the whole thing going incredibly well. All the mega-hotties in the gym would be stunned at my natural lifting prowess. I'd use a barbell to deter an armed intruder bent on terrorizing the weight room. I'd be promoted to Head Lifter and honored with a year's supply of Muscle Milk. *This could be my sport*, I thought. A sport that was, in fact, *for me*.

That's not how it happened. Not only had I never successfully lifted a barbell in my life; the weight room was also more crowded than I expected, full of people who looked like they knew exactly what they were doing. The squat racks were all occupied, so I googled "squat rack taken what to do????" Google advised me to ask the squat rack user for permission to "work in," which means you use the squat rack during their rest period. *All right*, I thought. *I'll ask to work in. No problem.*

The nearest squat rack was occupied by a good-looking guy in joggers. I tiptoed over to his rack, hands clasped behind my back, and stared at the floor reverently until he finished his dead lift. He looked at me sideways and dropped the barbell with a *clang*.

"Uh, yes, hello," I stuttered, bowing slightly. "Would it be at all possible for me to . . . work in?"

"I'm gonna be here a while," he said, which I took to mean no. I held both hands up and backed away apologetically, shuffling back to the part of the room I knew—the treadmills.

Getting there felt like Frogger. An auburn-haired woman crossed my path, delts bulging as she heaved a few kettlebells across the floor. "Sorry, sorry," I whispered, stepping around her. A man walked past me with a weight bench. "Sooooo sorry, excuse me," I muttered too quietly to be heard. I then trudged on the treadmill for a half hour until Joggers vacated his squat rack.

By the time I made it to the rack, I was fired up. I was ready to press a barbell above my head. I was ready to activate my lats. Just then, a man approached and asked if I was using the weight bench near my rack. I hunched like a submissive shih tzu and shook my head frantically. "All you, all you," I chirped, forgetting that I needed the bench for half of my lifts. He took the bench, and I spent another half hour awkwardly stretching and looking at my phone because I was too afraid to ask for the bench back.

By the time the man vacated the bench, I had spent an hour in the weight room and done exactly zero lifting. Finally, I dragged the bench back to my rack, narrowing my eyes like a territorial hawk every time someone came near, and began to lift. I consulted my little pink notebook and prepared for my first movement: the squat.

I had ripped a lifting plan off an obscure bodybuilding website, and the plan advised me to start with a sixty-five-pound squat. *Easy*, I thought, placing one ten-pound plate on either side of the bar. I then realized I didn't know which direction to face. I took a guess, squeezed my body into the back of the rack with my back facing the wall, and slipped under the bar. I tried to squat, but the bar clanged against the side of the rack. I put it back and tried going the other way. I then googled "where to stand squat rack" and realized I was standing the wrong way. I corrected that, and banged out three clumsy squats before taking a break, wiping my brow, and chugging some water.

After that came the dead lift. A dead lift is a tricky lift, capable of annihilating one's torso if performed incorrectly. I completed one rep, then stood up too fast and tweaked my lower back in a way that made me realize my twenties were basically over. Finally, I tried the bench press, a movement that felt so foreign I almost dropped the bar on my sternum. It was the least productive weight room session in modern history; still, I strode out of the room standing a bit taller than when I had entered. I was a *weight lifter* now.

Somehow, I stuck with it. That's partially because I realized you get to take big breaks in between sets, which allows me to scroll through my phone and stare open-mouthed at other gymgoers. I also realized that lifting weights requires eating, a fact that was totally foreign to me. In high school, my athletic classmates were always slugging chocolate milk and digging into huge quesadillas for lunch. But sports weren't *for me*; thus, eating with zeal to fuel my body wasn't *for me*. That had to change when I started weight lifting. Ultimately, it took a dietician's stern urging before I was able to nourish myself properly. And after six months of intentionally eating more than two thousand calories a day for the first time in my life, I slept the sleep of someone who's finally realized that they never really wanted to shrink. I wanted energy, and I wanted power, neither of which is attainable when one's sole focus is circling one's wrist with thumb and forefinger. Anyway, my thumb and forefinger are otherwise occupied at the moment. They're busy shoveling protein-enriched waffles into my gaping maw.

It's been a little over a year since the beginning of my iron-pumping journey. That 45-pound squat turned into a 125-pound squat, and I learned how to dead lift without throwing my back out. I eat well, I stand taller, and I feel like I'm really inhabiting my body for the first time. I am distinctly larger than when I started. My blood work is exceptional. This isn't to say that I've magically ditched three decades' worth of diet indoctrination. It still creeps up on me, especially when Instagram serves me the kind of sponsored ads that make me feel like a wretched hag. For a while, it was tiny ankle weights that promised to whittle away at lower body fat; recently, it's those cursed laxative teas. Proof that the algorithm is evil: muscled-out Instagram influencers inspired my lifting journey; now, two years later, my ad feed seems to suggest that my bulking has gone too far.

It seems counterintuitive, but part of lifting heavy things is being gentle with yourself. You can't force yourself to hoist 150 pounds in the air if your body isn't ready. Likewise, you can't force yourself to pretend that you're always completely in love with the way your body looks. But that's what I like about lifting: For the first time in my life, I feel happy about the things my body can *do*, rather than just the way it looks. For the record, I haven't heard a peep out of the uncle who complimented my skinny high school self. Maybe he's afraid that I'll throw him over my shoulder and squat his ass.

As I slip into my new, powerful, iron-pumping selfhood, I also take time to mourn the old me. I still get sad for her, she of the egg fasts and the seventeen-minute mile. I mourn the years I spent buying into what I now know to be a scam: the idea that I couldn't be an athlete because I didn't shoot out of my mother's womb with an Olympic luge sled in one hand and a gallon of Gatorade in the other. I mourn the years I could've spent enjoying the things my body *could* do instead of lamenting the things I thought it *couldn't*. And I feel sad for the kids who are still being tidily categorized into the seventeen-minute-mile club as some gym teacher tells them that only certain types of bodies are made to enjoy sports—and, worse, that only certain types of bodies are worth celebrating.

I am by no means a competitive athlete. I'm not terribly coordinated, and the PACER test would likely kill me. But I know how to chest press. I know how to squat. I climb challenging bouldering routes, and I go for runs when they feel good, and I don't get mad at myself when they don't. I've finally ditched the idea that exercise is supposed to feel bad, along with the lie that *sports aren't for me.* I've realized that the life I want doesn't allow for shrinking myself indefinitely. I want a life in which I may, at some point, step on someone's toes. I want to surround myself with people who cherish my perfectly average stature. I want to reject the idea of bowing and scraping and scrimping and shrinking to gain favor. I want to spread my arms wide and occupy the sunniest part of the sidewalk and maybe even *loom* a little. There's plenty of space to go around.

An Evening of Carnal Delights as Envisioned by My Ten-Year-Old Self

My lover is on his way. I know this because my mom just yelled downstairs, "Lillian, your lover is on his way!" I live in my parents' basement because I love them and they love me. We can just add on to the house if we decide we need more space for bulk Fruit Roll-Ups or whatever.

I ready myself, shaving my legs, arms, and butt. Then, I apply my perfume. I am thirty-two, which means I am old enough to spray a cloud of Britney Spears Circus perfume and then walk through it, letting the little droplets of perfume shower my bouncy curls and my big adult boobs. Finally, I rub the accompanying scented lotion on my hands because I have definitely grown out of my eczema at this point.

I hear a knock at the door. Titillated, I down the rest of my red wine—I'm always drinking red wine, because it tastes just like Communion grape juice—and flit to greet my lover. I'm always flitting.

I flit up the stairs to the front door and peek through the peephole. My parents let me paint the door baby blue because it's Justin Timberlake's favorite color as reported by the book *101 Amazing Justin Timberlake Facts*, by Frankie Taylor and Jack Goldstein. I open the door wide while also leaning sexily against the door frame, accentuating my nice boobs. "Hello," I say to my lover. "Welcome to my home."

"Hello," Orlando Bloom pants eagerly, striding into my home in full costume as Legolas from the first twenty minutes of *The Fellowship of the Ring* that I am allowed to watch. I take him wordlessly by the hand. We descend the fireman's pole that leads to my basement bedroom, which my dad was actually able to install pretty easily using a free how-to guide from Pottery Barn Teen. "Careful," Orlando Bloom moans cautiously. "Don't snag your round grown-up boobs on that fireman's pole."

We slide down the fireman's pole and land in my bedroom. Orlando Bloom whistles, impressed. "I like your old-fashioned popcorn machine," he says, gesturing to my old-fashioned popcorn machine. "Thank you," I say. "Please, help yourself to some old-fashioned popcorn as I slip into something more comfortable for my huge boobs." I give Orlando Bloom a wry smile as I coyly slip behind the bohemian beaded curtain that I got on sale at the Battlefield Mall.

Behind the beaded curtain, I flit out of my hooded shark robe and into a T-shirt emblazoned with Scooby Doo's Mystery Machine and the slogan "Original Love Machine." I step out from behind the curtain. Orlando Bloom staggers backward, clutching his chest.

"I love that T-shirt," he says tenderly. "It's from Limited Too," I purr erotically. "Oh, at the Battlefield Mall?" Orlando Bloom asks. I blush. "Yes, exactly."

I clap my hands and "Smooth" by Carlos Santana featuring Rob Thomas plays on a loop. Orlando Bloom tenderly tucks my hair behind my ears, slicking down the greasies and smoothing out my middle part, then licking his palms and tugging on the bottoms of the hairs to make them a little straighter.

"Let's get down to beeswax," Orlando Bloom murmurs hungrily. He parts my lips with his hand. "Close your eyes," he whispers before putting something tantalizingly sweet into my mouth.

"Oh my," I groan. "Is that . . ."

"That's right," Orlando Bloom whispers. "It's a Fruit Roll-Up from the Walmart Supercenter a few miles up the road."

I begin to shake uncontrollably as Orlando Bloom pushes me up against a wall. "Look at your nice boobs," he gasps. "Yeah," I say. "They sprouted when I was eleven and propelled me to instant popularity. If only I could write a letter to my ten-year-old self and let her know that these incredibly symmetrical, bouncing boobs were on the way. Boy, would she be relieved."

Orlando Bloom looks at me soulfully, and I can tell that he's about to kiss me the exact way I want to be kissed, which is by darting his tongue in and out of my mouth like a hermit crab. His body throbs because he knows how smart and good at making friendship bracelets I am. We rub our front parts together for a second.

"Wait," I cry daintily, holding up my right hand. "Before we go any further, I want you to know that I wear a purity ring. I wear this ring because I'm married to God until I marry my earthly husband."

Orlando Bloom is silent. He sits down and buries his head in his hands.

"I'm so sorry, lover," I weep. "But I, a thirty-two-year-old woman, am saving myself for marriage. This is a decision I made at an Evangelical sports camp when I was ten, and I have not doubted it once since."

Orlando Bloom raises his head. His eyes are filled with tears. He stands, strokes my cheek, and smiles.

He holds up his right hand. There, on his ring finger, is a thick silver band that reads LOVE WAITS.

"I have one, too," he says.

I have an absolutely explosive orgasm.

Welcome to Ass Planet

When you're a horny preteen in southwest Missouri in the mid-aughts, you've got two options to get your summertime rocks off:

Option 1: You can walk to the neighborhood pool, clench your butt cheeks, strut past the lifeguard stand, and give yourself a rip-roaring vulvar wedgie in an attempt to seduce a sixteen-year-old who drives a Dodge Neon and has permanent scarring from combining corrosive acne treatments.

Option 2: You can wait until your parents leave for work, leaving you home to babysit your kid siblings and watch reruns of *The Osbournes*. The second they leave, you can navigate to the smutty pay-per-view channels. You won't click on the channels, partly because you don't have a credit card, and partly because your semi-Pentecostal grandmother taught you that God can see what you're doing at all times. Instead, you'll just scroll through the channel titles, whispering as you read them. *"Big Titted Brunette Gets Spanking Surprise,"* you'll murmur, shimmying out of your pajama pants. *"Schoolgirls Get Nasty at Unsanctioned Water Park,"* you'll pant, scooting back and forth on the polyester couch. *"WELCOME TO ASS PLANET,"* you'll squeak as your crotch snaps open and shut like a turtle's beak.

As soon as I hit puberty, I chose Option 2. I became the Lewis & Clark of Ass Planet, studying pornographic taxonomy the way my classmates studied the periodic table. I couldn't tell you the chemical symbol for beryllium, but I could tell you which channels featured butthole and which ones showcased motorboat action. I lingered in the pay-per-view channels until I got my first MP3 player. That's when I learned about a mysterious download process called torrenting.

Instead of begging to use my dad's credit card to purchase Ace of Base's *Happy Nation*, I learned to navigate sites full of pirated material to build my personal music library, free of charge. The best part: You could torrent pretty much anything. You could torrent Usher's latest, but you could also pad your cabinet of carnal curiosities by torrenting low-resolution videos of women with gravity-defying bosoms doing weird sex stuff.

I still don't know how torrenting works, but I liked to imagine the digital porn stars breaking into a million tiny Mike Teavee–sized pieces that flew, humping vigorously, into the air before landing in my family's computer hard drive. There I could enjoy them for a few days until the PC crashed and I had to tell my mom that, nope, I had no clue why we had so many ads for penis pills and online poker on our otherwise pristine desktop.

Eventually, my parents got wise and forbade me from torrenting. But I still had plenty to do, because this was 2008, and a mottled human candlestick named Mark Zuckerberg was making history with this thing called Facebook. On Facebook, you could wish your aunt a happy birthday, share the news of your upcoming promotion to taekwondo purple belt, and post unflattering pictures of your best friend under the caption "SUMMA 4EVA—randomest gurl I know XD."

The type of image one might use to pursue internet flirtation in 2008.

But for me, Facebook represented a virtual buffet of pubescent sexual expression. That primarily involved a chat app called Hot-OrNot. HotOrNot started as a communal activity: Cassidy passed Melanie a note that read "HotOrNot after skewl?" at which point Melanie flipped open her yellow Motorola Sidekick and texted Jen. "hey we're doin HotOrNot after skewl." Then Jen leaned over to me in English class and whispered, "HotOrNot after school," at which point the teacher flipped around from the blackboard and looked at us with the beady eyes of a great horned owl.

The concept of HotOrNot was simple. Think of it as an early Tinder, minus the location pinpointing. First, you completed your profile. (Mine was punctuated by two mirror selfies I took on my digital camera—flash *on*—and one panel that just read "Child of God" in hot pink bubble letters.) Then, you clicked through other HotOrNot users and classified them as Hot or Not Hot. This was an excellent group activity, the sort of voyeuristic sleepover fun that paved the way for shrieking at anonymous penises on Chatroulette. If you marked someone "Hot" and they reciprocated, you could message each other. That's how I met my first great love: Ibrahim, a Moroccan man of indiscriminate age.

I had no business messing around on HotOrNot. I was thirteen, and absolutely not hot, but Ibrahim didn't know either of those things. (He thought I was fourteen.) On Facebook I was a glamorous, asthma-inhaler-toting Liza Minnelli, and the world was my underground cabaret. Later, I'd figure out that posting the lyrics to Sting's "Englishman in New York" would *not* get me kissed the way I desperately want to be kissed, which was in a way that is wet but somehow also dry. But at this point I had no reason to doubt Ibrahim when he dished out compliments, remarking on my hair (short with chunky highlights), eyes (ringed in purple eyeliner from Claire's), and lips (stretched in a grimace that revealed braces with yellow and green bands, which formed a snot-colored ladder across my teeth).

Ibrahim and I talked for hours, breaking my personal record for longest HotOrNot chat. The previous record holder was the thirty-something man who asked for a mirror selfie of me holding my retainer in my hand. I sent it, because I was bold and cosmopolitan and also didn't know what a fetish was.

It wasn't long before Ibrahim and I took things to AOL Instant Messenger. I, a hopelessly horny thirteen-year-old, spent hours chatting with this internet stranger, he of the shaved head and the flexed bicep and the mysterious camera angle that revealed one eye like he was a sea monster looking in through the porthole of love. Ibrahim was the Moby-Dick of internet conquests, and I had ensnared him with my cool screen name: ikick4christ, an homage to my identity as an Evangelical martial artist. Our conversations were loaded with passion and intrigue.

Basketball2085: hello my baby how are u doin
smoke all day party all night

ikick4christ: bonjour handsome! xD just herd a song that
made me think of u

~*~*~* There's only two types of people in the world:
The ones that entertain, and the ones that observe
——Britney Spears *~*~*~

Basketball2085: i love rap
smoke all day party all night

ikick4christ: here it is . . . . xx **[download file:
AshleeSimpsonPiecesOfMe.mp4]**

~*~*~* There's only two types of people in the world:
The ones that entertain, and the ones that observe
——Britney Spears *~*~*~

Basketball2085: baby how would you like me to kiss you
smoke all day party all night

ikick4christ: mmmmm up on da wall

~*~*~* There's only two types of people in the world:
The ones that entertain, and the ones that observe
——Britney Spears *~*~*~

Basketball2085: mmm
smoke all day party all night

ikick4christ: mmmmmmmmmm

~*~*~* There's only two types of people in the world:
The ones that entertain, and the ones that observe
—Britney Spears *~*~*~

Ibrahim never gave me that unforgettable kiss up on da wall.
That honor went to Miles Campbell, who cupped my right boob in
my parents' basement while we watched *Pulp Fiction*. Miles was a
singular character, defined by three distinct actions:

1. Inexplicably bringing his beach towel to our *Pulp
   Fiction* date, an act which still causes my parents
   great confusion. "Did he think he was going to the
   neighborhood pool?" my mom occasionally asks,
   bewildered. Truly, I do not know.

2. Mailing me a burned CD that contained one song and one
   song alone: "Closer" by Nine Inch Nails.

3. Years later, emailing me the first chapter of his
   manuscript. That remains the first and only time I've
   seen the words "I palmed her begging ass" typed out in a
   Word document. Until now, I guess.

But before Miles, there was *Ibrahim*. As with many great ro-
mances, Ibrahim and I exchanged I Love Yous after about a week
of meaningless pleasantries and clumsy dirty talk. I was the first of
my friends to say those words to a man, and I felt very self-satisfied
and worldly—so worldly that I agreed to use precious international
minutes to call Ibrahim on my Nokia flip phone. (He told me that he
wanted to hear me say "I love you" in my sexy voice. He could tell

I had a sexy voice because "my eyes danced" in my profile photo, which was likely the result of a motor tic.)

I called Ibrahim on a Wednesday after school, perched atop a concrete table at the neighborhood Sonic after slamming a few rounds of Coney dogs with my friends. I shivered with anticipation as I dialed in Ibrahim's international phone number on the chubby little phone I got for my thirteenth birthday. My friend Cassidy took out her glitter retainer, stuffed half a Coney into her mouth, and chanted, "Call him, call him," between bites of wiener.

After a few rings, he picked up.

I gasped and nearly dropped the phone, in disbelief that I was connecting with my life partner over a scratchy international connection.

"Hello, baby?" he yelled over the static.

"I'm here!" I crowed, knowing that we only had a few minutes because international calling from my dinky phone was exorbitantly expensive.

"I want to hear you say it, baby," he said.

"Okay, okay," I replied squeakily. "ILOVEYOU."

"No, say it to me in the language of LOOOOOVE," he begged. "Say it in French. Je t'aaaaaime."

"UH OKAY JAH-TIM," I chortled, nearly throwing up because of a feeling I thought was eroticism but was actually just deep, deep embarrassment. I snapped my Nokia closed and emptied a box of tater tots while my idiot friends fell over laughing.

A week later, my dad saw an international call to Morocco on the family phone bill. He took my phone, sat me down on our eternally damp basement couch, and told me it was time to break things off with the love of my life. This came at the worst time possible, given that Ibrahim had just proposed to me over AIM. I had heartily accepted and was very much looking forward to flying to Morocco to have his mother and sister adorn my hands with henna tattoos. Alas, I was grounded. I had also developed a crush on someone in my Outdoor Awareness class. When I broke the news to Ibrahim over AIM, he replied in all caps:

Basketball2085: U BROKE MY HEA
RT!!
smoke all day party all night

I didn't end up getting with the kid in my Outdoor Awareness class, who expressed his disinterest by looming over my desk and yelling "WILL YOU SHUT THE *HELL* UP" as I hummed a song from the *Princess Diaries* soundtrack. Instead, I took up with a young man who had an *Eraserhead* haircut and a prominent position on the city's finest high school drum line. On our first date, he took me to see Mark Wahlberg's *The Happening* and paid for my Sno-Caps. On our second date, he invited me to sit on his roof and listen to a Christian heavy metal album in its entirety. On our third date, he became my first ever real-life boyfriend, despite the fact that we had nothing in common, relied entirely on our parents for transportation, and each had a monthly cap of twenty text messages.

Our romance lasted all of three months. After a few weeks, I started to realize that we didn't actually like one another—we just liked doing over-the-pants stuff and sending :P :P :P emoticons back and forth. I hated his metal music; he thought I was a snob. His intense mom made me uncomfortable; my mom's frenetic kitchen disco dancing made him squirm. But, as far as I could tell, a committed relationship had nothing to do with mutual respect or enjoyment. *Seventeen* and *Cosmo* headlines screamed out ways to "Keep Your Man Interested" and the romantic entanglements I saw on *MTV reality shows* were pretty much entirely based on mutual hatred. The way I saw it, love took *work*. I was willing to put in that work because I had a *boyfriend*, and he was *very tall*.

Until Eraserhead got a haircut. I knew it was over when he showed up to my parents' house for an afternoon dry hump, his hair shaped into a sort of mushroom cloud formation. It was shaved on the bottom, trimmed in the middle, and swelling out at the very top in a style that made his head look like a small vat of French onion soup. I could handle our mutual disdain, but a boyfriend with bad hair seemed detrimental to my long-term student government prospects. I shot Eraserhead a text, told him I was ending things to pursue musical theater more aggressively, and waited for the fallout. He actually took the breakup pretty well—until my dad woke up early on a Sunday morning, shuffled to the end of the driveway to pick up the paper, and screamed:

"IT'S A GODDAMN DICK!"

My mom and I rushed outside to discover a giant penis painted on our garage door. The culprit had painted several smaller penises, one mid-ejaculation, directly on my bedroom window. No matter how hard we scrubbed, the penises didn't come off. Eraserhead, along with a few of his drum-line friends, had drawn the dicks in shoe polish. The prank forced my parents to install a new garage door and prompted my dad to sit his Texan ass in a lawn chair on our driveway, machete across his lap, just waiting to boogie with a teenage outlaw.

Much to my dad's dismay, my taste in mates remained poor. After Eraserhead, there was the *Rob Dyrdek's Fantasy Factory* superfan who sped away after accidentally crashing his pickup truck into my neighbor's car. I dismissed this as fine. ("Go Easy on Your Man!") Next came the spirited lad who had the kind of vigorous physical energy that leads young men into the sultry clutches of parkour. I spent our relationship running after him like a babysitter chasing a toddler on a pool deck. ("Keep Him Entertained!") Our romance concluded in a monster fight in which he accused me of being boring and I accused him of trying to sabotage my run for student body president because he wore purple knockoff UGG boots to school as a joke.

After that, I let a twenty-two-year-old Marine recruiter take me on a lunch date to Panera Bread. He had obtained my number in the worst possible way: by sneaking a peek at my school-issued schedule, which he, along with his brothers in arms, had volunteered to distribute on the first day of class. I barely acknowledged the Marines that day, failing to register the uniformed men lurking in my low-income high school trying to get kids to join up in exchange for free USB drives. Still, I was sickeningly flattered to receive his text that afternoon. I agreed to the Panera date; I ordered macaroni and cheese in a bread bowl, an entrée that would likely kill me at this point in my life. After lunch, he tried to finger-blast me in a Walmart parking lot, which I would've allowed if he hadn't suddenly pulled back, ashen, and proclaimed, "I have a wife."

The incident with the Marine should have been my first indication that something was awry. True, my prefrontal cortex was still in development, and my hippocampus was addled by a unique drug cocktail meant to suppress my twitchy, OCD-ridden nature. But the fact remained: I was open to dating a clumsily predatory adult man with whom I had nothing in common, who prowled around area high schools looking for underage prospects and drove a tiny pickup truck with a Calvin Pissing sticker on the fender. Why? Because I hadn't just been noticed; I had been *selected*.

In that moment, I boarded the SS *Power Imbalance* and chucked my own interests, sexual desires, and general hopes for affable human companionship out of the nearest porthole. A dude clad in *bona fide fatigues* found me attractive. It proved that I was passing as the likable, attractive, magnetic person I wanted to be. Believing those things about myself wasn't enough; I needed confirmation from the outside. And it didn't matter that my suitor was a huge creep who almost certainly slept with a makeshift beach towel blackout curtain tacked over his bedroom window. It was an honor just to be nominated.

By the time I made it to senior prom, I had wrangled a very respectable high school boyfriend who boasted a perfect ACT score and centaur-level hairy butt cheeks. He asked me to prom on a bike ride, which was endearing, but disappointing considering that my friend's date had requested the honor of her presence by placing candles in her front yard and accidentally setting her cul-de-sac ablaze. Regardless, I accepted. I picked out a heinous peach-colored dress and, about a week before the big day, headed to the hair salon for an updo consultation. The stylist was stern, with the kind of perfectly straight bangs that could cover years' worth of forehead flatiron burns. She flipped through the photos I cut out of *Seventeen* for inspiration ("Be His Dream Prom Date!"), nodded, and started brushing my hair.

Suddenly, she dropped her comb. She held her hands up, backed away, and told my mom to get me out of there before anyone saw. "You have to leave now," she bellowed, pointing to the half-dozen tiny bugs creeping across the comb. My disgusting head was absolutely crawling with lice.

My best guess is that I picked it up from a high school play. The play had concluded the week before, and most of our costume budget went to a box of communal stocking caps meant to *unite the ensemble.* But I didn't have time to point fingers. I only had a few days to battle the creepy-crawlies on my scalp if I had any chance of making out in my boyfriend's giant basement beanbag chair after prom. Over the course of the next week, I scorched my scalp with every lice-killing shampoo Walgreens had in stock, screaming while my poor mother combed nit poison into my long, coarse hair. It wasn't long before I passed the bugs on to my younger sister, an even louder screamer than I. We endured four days of hourly nit combing when my mom brought out the hillbilly remedy: painting our heads with thick globs of mayonnaise and sending us to bed in sticky, stinking shower caps.

The mayo treatment worked. I fashioned an elaborate braid at the last minute and cruised to our Willy Wonka–themed prom in my lover's bitchin' Volvo. I danced to maybe three songs and spent the rest of the night eating Nerds Ropes in my eighty-pound dress. It was the best night ever.

My high school Lice King and I parted ways a few months into college, which was just as well because I was about to discover wine coolers. This led to an obscene sequence of suitors, including a random party makeout that sent me screaming into Planned Parenthood because I was convinced I had picked up chlamydia of the tonsils. (The nurse laughed at me as I cried and tried to explain that she didn't understand; we used *tongue*.) Shortly after, I got my kicks with a swimmer whose idea of personal hygiene was a quick dip in a chlorinated pool.

After that, I ended up entangled with an upperclassman with a long Eastern European last name, a wry smile, and a tiny, tiny butt. After countless shots of Burnett's Blueberry vodka, Tiny Butt invited me to his fraternity formal. I gleefully accepted, texting him a few days later to confirm attire (semiformal, which meant squeezing my flesh into some kind of tube) and the food situation (a hibachi steakhouse, which meant I'd be sitting on the floor while squeezed into my semiformal tube). I didn't hear back until the day of the formal, when I texted him one more time to confirm, to which he replied with a quick "yup."

I met him at the restaurant, where I managed to sit and eat without splitting my fancy tube. A few hours later, we arrived at a low-end wine bar for the dance. After about half an hour of rubbing our private parts together to the musical stylings of Ke$ha, Tiny Butt spun me around and leaned in. I closed my eyes, ready to ram my tongue down his throat. His face passed my lips and went straight to my ear. I heard him belch lightly, then whisper, "I don't remember inviting you to this dance."

Turns out that he had a serious alcohol problem and was blackout drunk when he extended the invite. It was only after I texted him earlier that week that he was able to confirm with my sorority sisters that he had, in fact, asked me out.

I assured him this was not a problem, as I was very cool. ("5 Ways to Distract Him While You Cry!") Three hours later, I found myself covered in his saliva after a session of heavy petting in his crumb-filled bed. I fell asleep with my cheek pressed into a half-eaten bag of wasabi peas and woke up in the wee hours to a piercing ray of sunlight and the thunderous snores of his three roommates. The situation didn't look good in the light of day, so I decided to sneak away before making eye contact with anyone in a half-mile radius.

As I got dressed, I realized that I couldn't find my underpants. I guess I should call them panties, because they were red and lacy and sexy and made my butt look like a tight little circus peanut. These were *nice underpants*—but his roommates had started to stir and I needed to escape. I abandoned the mission and trudged home without my intimates.

A few hours later, I smeared CoverGirl foundation over my hickeys and joined my friends in the dining hall to discuss the night's events. They were livid. This was the year 2012, so we sought revenge the only way we knew how: by launching a Twitter-Tumblr crossover campaign centered on the hashtag #PantySnifferSighting. We convinced ourselves that my panties weren't just missing; they had been *stolen* by my date, who was a big, panty-sniffing pervert. For the next week, every time we saw my date on campus, we'd send out a #PantySnifferSighting alert on Twitter.

This encounter taught me three things: first, that fraternities are evil; second, that I can spot a panty sniffer a mile away. The final lesson from Tiny Butt Panty Sniffer was less straightforward. Like Unhygienic Swimmer, Mouth Chlamydia, Marine Recruiter, Ibrahim, and all the rest, Tiny Butt Panty Sniffer assumed I'd be cool with . . . pretty much anything. Inform this young lady that you don't remember asking her on this date? No big deal—she'll be cool with it.

Steal a high schooler's phone number while you're supposed to be recruiting ill-informed young men to die for their country? Go for it—she's chill. Cover your ex-girlfriend's garage door in shoe polish penises, costing her family many, many dollars? She'll be fine. (Her dad won't.)

When unyielding chillness is the baseline, garbage treatment always follows. This is a problem for those of us who've learned to define our self-worth by our desirability, an approach that makes standing up for oneself impossible. If, for some reason, you find yourself feeling upset about the garbage treatment you've endured, it's probably on you.

My romantic history reads a little like a sculptor's artistic statement. *The artist wishes to convey rebirth with every passing flirtation.* It's honestly impressive, the way I've hacked away at myself time and time again, taking a few months in between to slap on some wet clay before dipping into another relationship with someone I didn't even like. For a sculptor to complete her masterpiece, she must chisel away at all the bits that don't fit, leaving behind something smooth and lifeless. That's the way I saw myself—covered in bits that didn't quite fit with the vision these men hoped to project upon me. For years, my likes, dislikes, and sexual predilections took the shape of a mottled statue of David; I, a bored and codependent Renaissance artist. I chiseled away at my own musical tastes and replaced them with Jawbreaker or R.E.M., whatever preferences fell in line with the boyfriend of the day. I slapped on layers of basketball trivia and faux vegetarianism. I took the shape of a supportive football player's girlfriend, the perfect fraternity formal date, the long-suffering significant other who serves as financial benefactor, housekeeper, and therapist to a grown man to stave off his withering passive aggression.

There are two problems with sculpting as an art form. First, noses are hard. Second, you only have so much clay to work with. If you cut away too much, you'll have to start over entirely. That's what I had to do. I was in my early twenties, sitting on the living room floor after yet another breakup. My boyfriend had moved out, leaving me with half-empty bookshelves and a patchy gallery wall. I didn't feel sad; just embarrassed. I didn't recognize myself. My sexual and romantic awakening began with a fierce pursuit of my own pleasure via smutty pay-per-view and ended with complete self-abandonment. My peers were striking out on their own, beginning these rich, full lives; meanwhile, I had no clue who I was. I had spent too much time contorting myself to please others. I was too preoccupied with *being chosen*; I had disregarded my own right to *choose*.

I did a good job of performing confidence and self-sufficiency, but I suspect that those closer to me saw something different— someone who had molted beyond recognition in the process of dating people who made her feel bad. I didn't know what kind of music I was into. I didn't know which movies or books I wanted to consume in the privacy of my own apartment. I didn't even know my favorite color. This uncertainty wasn't the result of long-term abuse or manipulation, although my love life has occasionally been smudged by both. I had simply compromised my sense of self in an attempt to become worthy of love. I was so convinced of my own terminal inadequacy that I never stopped to wonder if I was having a good time.

Fortunately, I've kicked the habit. It takes practice; I still experience mild dread when I tell my partner that I don't want to accompany him to a concert at 10 p.m. on a Tuesday. It's difficult to proclaim that you are worthy of love, zero chiseling required. It's terrifying to be yourself in relationships—but it's more terrifying to think about a future that involves wedging your personality behind the door in a trench coat, *Babadook*-style, only coming out under the cover of darkness for fear of scaring someone off. Relationships take compromise, but any relationship that requires chiseling isn't worth the cost of admission. To claim love—and, in a way, to offer it with any sort of authenticity—I must fling my sculpting hammer into the sea, gesturing wildly at myself and screaming, "DONE! DONE! FINISHED!" If I take future artistic liberties with my personhood—shaving off an inch of Shania Twain fandom, perhaps, or chipping away at my bias against green olives—it'll be for me. No one else. Not a mottled Marine recruiter, nor a cruel collegian; not even my current partner, who'd never ask me to tinker anyway. I am exhausted, but I am here, unchiselable when it matters most. I am the master of my own Ass Planet, the ruthless forsaker of passive-aggressive ex-boyfriends and unsatisfying flings. I am once again covered in clay, comfortably cushioned by all my own contradictions.

I'm here. All of me.

I'm a Clog Bitch Now

Rachel? So good to see you! Yeah, I'm doing really well—I'm a clog bitch now. As in, I only wear clogs. Look down. See? There they are.

Are my feet cold? Honestly, I can't even feel them. They're permanently calloused and gnarled after weeks of walking on a block of wood. That's the life of a clog bitch, baby.

Let me be clear: Being a clog bitch is more than just wearing clogs. It's a lifestyle. Being a clog bitch means I repurpose my partner's used floss into quirky holiday garlands. Tunics? I wear those now. All clog bitches do. Kate Bush? UGH, YES. The Knife? Fiona Apple? Bitch, I'm WEARING clogs, aren't I? Look down.

As a clog bitch, I go positively bananas for lavender-scented shit. I grow lemons in the dank alley next to my brownstone. I make my own oat milk using a thin cloth that I embroidered with the sound waves generated by Björk's "Jóga." Once again, I AM a clog bitch.

I own so many rugs now. Collecting rugs is a thing that clog bitches do. Sometimes, I'll peel up one rug only to find another rug underneath it.

Being a clog bitch means that I carry an unreasonably large

hand-felted bag I picked up in Barcelona. Once again, this bag is insanely huge. I need it in case I have to pick up more clogs on my commute. I can fit about three pairs in here.

As a clog bitch, I love to educate people on the dangers of non-organic household items—like paraffin candles. The first time I put on the clogs, I was immediately like, um, paraffin? What in the FUCK? Here, have a wool dryer ball. I have some in this gigantic FUCKING bag.

Lunch? No, thanks—clog bitches like myself only eat photos of Chloë Sevigny. It's nice because I can eat a photo of Chloë and my body physically cannot digest it, which means I can shit it out and eat it again. This cycle goes on for a few days, which reduces a LOT of waste. You'd be surprised.

A cool thing that happens now that I'm a clog bitch is I can pull Joan Didion quotes out of my mouth. They're printed on small slips of paper in my digestive tract. All I have to do is unhinge my jaw a little and one or two will pop out from under my tongue. Here, look. Oh, that's from *The Year of Magical Thinking*! That's a good one.

Clog is love. Clog is life. clog good. clog happy. clog joy. eat clog for breakfast. when me no have clog me body systems shut down one by one. clog keep me warm at night. when god happy with me god rain down clog. clog clog clog clog clog clog clog clog

Anyway, I'm thinking of becoming a crochet bitch next!

I'm a Clog Bitch Now (Pt. 2)

I'm being haunted by a denim newsboy hat. The first time I saw it, I was at a coffee shop. I glanced up from my crossword and saw a flash of dusty blue through the window. "It can't be," I gasped, flying to the door just in time to see the jaunty cap cross the street. I saw it again a few weeks later, in a Gap ad on the subway. The model's eyes seemed to follow me as I stared, the blood draining from my face. Since then, I've seen the hat around corners, down dark alleys, and in the split second before a city bus crosses my path. The denim newsboy hat is taunting me, as if to say: "I'm back, baby."

It's not just the hat. A slew of Y2K fashion relics have appeared from beyond the grave recently, summoned by unsuspecting tween TikTokers and enterprising eBay merchants hoping to make a killing on used platform flip-flops. Those of us who came of age in the aughts know the truth: that the 2000s were the most sinister aesthetic era since the age of the corset. Now we're being forced to watch as the next generation invites our vanquished low-rise demons back into the realm of the living. "It's been twenty years," we moan shakily, bony fingers clutching our old patchwork jeans. No one listens to us, the withered harbingers of doom.

I hit puberty in the mid-aughts. Even so, for me, the fashion of the day was largely out of reach. The scarves were skinny, but the belts were wide. The highlights were chunky, but the models were rail-thin. Belly chains clanged across pop stars' nubile midsections. Disney Channel starlets wore dresses *over* jeans. Meanwhile, I couldn't wear layers of any kind—including dresses over jeans—because my school didn't have air-conditioning and blazed so hot that little beads of sweat trickled into my knockoff K-Swiss sneakers. I desperately wanted a velour tracksuit, but my mom didn't like the idea of emblazoning the word JUICY across my twelve-year-old ass. I couldn't wear Von Dutch trucker hats because my dad thought they were trashy. (My dad also would not abide Livestrong bracelets because Lance Armstrong seemed vaguely liberal.)

And sure, I could've purchased a tasteful crocheted poncho from the JCPenney Juniors section—but a tasteful crocheted poncho somewhat limits one's arm movements, making it extremely hard to raise your hands and scream, "Wait! You forgot your messenger bag!" if you happened to see teen heartthrob Adam Brody walking down the street without his messenger bag. A girl had to be *ready*.

Hindered by the unfortunate limitations of aughts fashion, I turned to comfort. From about 2002 to 2005, I refused to wear anything even mildly uncomfortable, relying instead on banded sweatpants and oversize tees. Jeans were off the table. Sneakers were purchased one size too large to avoid toe compression. Underpants were huge, baggy briefs of the Hanes persuasion, worn beneath the waist for ultimate flexibility. The photos from this period are heinous—but, damn, I was comfy.

I'd like to say that my turn to comfort was some bold, forward-thinking rejection of the restrictive fashions of the day; a political statement against the belly-chained masses. In reality, it was just the first time I was allowed to dress myself. My mom dressed me for the first few years of my life, sliding my pudgy body into jaunty little denim onesies with matching sailor hats. I was the only kid—my younger siblings didn't come along until I was in elementary school—and my mom had a field day with bows, barrettes, and glittery sandals. I don't remember that part of my life, although my mom swears I was compliant. "You didn't say a word until you hit nine or ten," she tells me over the phone. "Then it was all stretchy waistbands and thin socks. You were very picky about your socks."

From that point on, I turned to function over fashion. I reached for clothes that allowed me to skitter across the playground with banshee-like abandon. I experimented with different personas—a sporty phase wherein I wore the same mesh basketball shorts for days on end; a cowgirl cosplay phase that involved studded jeans and functional boots that barely fit over my beefy calves. There was even a very brief bohemian phase, which involved much appropriation of moccasins.

Look closely for culturally insensitive footwear.

During each of these phases, comfort was key. On the rare occasion that I wore something more restrictive—a preppy button-down here, a homecoming dress there—I'd shed my clothes as soon as I got home, leaving them in a pile on the floor as I shimmied into a giant *Sanford and Son* T-shirt. I'd sigh in relief, swinging my limbs and releasing my clenched gut until I started to feel like myself again.

Some people feel at home in slinky cocktail dresses and crisp suits. I've always felt most at home in a roomy garment. I spent my college years trying to ignore that fact, squeezing myself into uncomfortable clothing long after exposed thongs went out of fashion. From age eighteen to twenty-one, I acquired a small pile of god-awful Lilly Pulitzer prints, Ralph Lauren polo minidresses, and fake pearl necklaces, all purchased from a Branson outlet mall in an attempt to keep up with my wealthier peers. I scored a pair of knockoff Ray-Bans from a street vendor and wore them around my neck on a printed neoprene sunglass strap. I teased my hair in ways designed to mimic the deftly bouffanted sorority women of the fifties and sixties, that golden age when Greek life was a turbocharged shuttle into matrimony.

None of this came naturally. I tumbled into college with a wardrobe of commemorative tees, swishy running shorts, and crunchy hiking sandals, all standard fare for the students at my unfussy high school. That served me just fine until midway through my freshman year, when I stumbled into a fraternity house and found myself sucked into a swirling Xibalba of seersucker and chevron. Old Crow Medicine Show's "Wagon Wheel" blared as I was fed shot after shot of Burnett's Blueberry vodka. I spun around in circles, drunk for the first time and dazzled by my vaguely *Stepford Wives*–ian surroundings. I leaned against a wall with my roommate, watching as boys in idiotic bow ties chatted with manicured girls. The heels were high, the bronzer was stripey, and the overall demeanor was about as scummy as you can get. Thinking back, it was pure hell—but I wanted in.

Maybe it was hormones, propelling me crotch-first into a crowd of faux sophisticates chugging Keystone. Maybe I was shell-shocked in the presence of genuine wealth. This was Ozarks wealth, built on tractor-trailer patents and plumbing fortunes. But it excited me, especially since the closest thing to a country club I'd seen was my grandpa's Elks Lodge, where I chugged Shirley Temples and played Texas Hold'em in a thick haze of old-man cigarette smoke. More likely it was the appeal of infamy, of belonging to an exclusive club. I closed my eyes and saw myself striding across campus, leaving a cascade of whispers in my wake. "That's Lillian Stone," a wide-eyed classmate would whisper. "I heard she enjoyed a tipple of blueberry Burnett's with the heir to the Dick's Plumbing Fortune."

I spent the next few years shellacking myself with a hard-earned sheen of sorority luster. I had squirreled away some cash from my summer job at the shaved-ice stand, which I used on chevron-printed shift dresses and nude heels. Most of my school supplies featured preppy pink whales. For a very brief moment in time, I changed my laptop password to "audreyhepburn."

All of this to earn the favor of the most heinous guys and dolls on campus. I teetered around in ankle-breaking espadrilles, genuflecting as I watched fraternity boys congregate at College Republicans conventions and dispose of girls like roadkill. I stabbed my scalp with bobby pins and permanently compromised my blood–brain barrier via hairspray inhalation, convinced that I could peacock my way into their hearts.

As my heels got higher, my standards for camaraderie got lower. I lost touch with my high school best friend and clung instead to a group of girls who blacked out and screamed obscenities at each other most nights. I laughed gamely every time a hammered upperclassman slung an arm over my shoulder and called me his bitch. I was *in*. That is, until the fraternity bell tolled for me, the same way it tolls for any woman with a pulse. After one particularly heinous drunken night, I was tossed out on my chevron-printed ass. Later that night, I sloshed back to my apartment, glanced at myself in the mirror, and straightened the bow in my carefully curled hair. I looked like a doll, and I felt like one, too—a plaything thrown out by a gaggle of spoiled children. I ripped the bow out of my hair, threw it in the trash, and passed out with my makeup on.

Shortly after trashing the hair bow, I graduated and sped away from my college campus. I was determined to bury the persona I had been trying to inhabit for four years. I was embarrassed, and rightly so—I had suffocated myself under layers of cheap foundation and stashed my personality in a stylish clutch, all for the benefit of some of the worst people I've ever met. Desperately in need of a personal rebrand, I decided my only option was complete physical transformation.

My initial thought was to join the punk scene, but I worried that I'd get laughed out of any decent DIY house. I pictured the door guy sniffing me from head to toe, then sending me packing after picking up the lingering stench of discount Polo Ralph Lauren. Scared of punk judgment, I went the opposite direction: I spent my first grown-up paycheck on a haul from ModCloth, the go-to fashion source for twee teachers, cat ladies, and intense femmes who are worryingly into *Alice in Wonderland*.

I vacuum-sealed myself into a cutesy Peter Pan–collared blouse, tucked a pair of lacy midcalf socks into my new brogues, donned a pair of musical note earrings, and assessed my progress in the mirror. One thing seemed out of place. I fingered my blond ringlets, periodically highlighted at a high-dollar blowout salon in keeping with the sorority style of the day. This wasn't the hair of a ModCloth rewards cardholder. This was the hair of a fraternity devotee who hadn't yet caught on to her own disposability. It was time for a visit to my uncle.

By day, my uncle cuts hair out of a pirate-themed salon. By night, he plays coed roller derby and thrashes to industrial music. He's six feet of hairy brawn, with an enormous jester tattoo on one thigh and giant hands somehow capable of wielding tiny trimming shears. The perfect person with whom to entrust my new look.

I plopped into his chair, which was sandwiched between a curtain of Mardi Gras beads and a standing dryer draped in iridescent purple fabric. "What are we thinking, sis?" he asked, fastening the cape around my neck with shocking grace for a dude of Hulk Hogan stature. I showed him the ModCloth website, a six-by-six grid of models with platinum blonde pixie cuts and blunt bangs. I pointed at a model with a tidy platinum chop that fell just beneath her chin. She smirked at the camera, displaying a small handbag shaped like a pineapple. *She wouldn't be caught dead in a fraternity house*, I thought. I tapped her photo and looked up at my uncle. "That one," I said, spinning around to face the back wall.

Three hours later, my uncle rotated me back toward the mirror. He glanced down at me guiltily. "Just a heads-up," he murmured. "This came out, uh, pretty ashy."

It wasn't ashy—my hair was blue.

Not his fault; I had dyed my naturally dark-blond hair beyond recognition in college, and we had gone slightly too cool with the toner. That left my hair a sickly shade of grayish blue, almost like brain matter blue. I squinted at myself. It wasn't what I had in mind, but it did advance my descent in alt-girl territory. I left the salon and went straight to Walgreens for a can of spray-in blue hair dye. Back at home, I flipped my head over and coated my hair in the stuff until it dried to an aquamarine crust. I looked like a rockabilly Smurf. It was perfect.

I completed the look with a pair of neon orange clogs, which I still have. Honestly, *neon* barely captures their fluorescence. What's the word for an eyeball-annihilating color that lands somewhere between a crossing guard's safety vest and a traffic cone? How do I describe this specific shade of orange that makes poison dart frogs look like tapioca-colored cave creatures? Suffice to say, this is not a color found in nature. This is the Devil's orange, vulgar enough to tear a hole in the universe and summon a long-dormant Titan from beneath the earth's crust. It's a shade that grants the wearer a certain sense of untouchable ridiculousness, especially when combined with the innate quirkiness of Scandinavian footwear. Wearing the neon orange clogs sends a message: "I could be the most stylish person you've ever met, or I could've just murdered my neighbor while blaring Jefferson Starship. Or both."

The clogs live in the back of my closet, an area I've reserved for detritus from my quirky era. There you'll find the ModCloth haul, punctuated by a polyester maxi dress covered in a garish tomato print. The dress has puffed sleeves and a small Crystal Light stain above the left breast. I wore it to my brother's high school graduation, forever enshrining both the dress and the stain in the Stone family history books.

Next to the tomato dress is an A-line skirt covered in vertical circus tent stripes. I wore it once or twice before I realized it made me look like a steampunk Ms. Frizzle. Also left over from that era are a pile of thrifted enamel earrings, a T-shirt that reads BABE WITH THE POWER, and a decorative pin featuring Tommy Pickles in the little red suit from *Twin Peaks*.

Just as the Russian Revolution was a response to the unabashed decadence of the czars, my quirky phase was a response to the humiliation of my preppy phase. I wanted to send a message: that I had grown, that I had shed my pick-me husk, that I was finally coming into my own—as if my own empowerment derived from a pair of earrings shaped like shrimp.

I hadn't really come into my own. I didn't even know what my own *was*. My entire approach to fashion was reactionary. Just like my fake-pearl phase was a reaction to the social pressures of my tiny college, my quirky phase was a reaction to the degradation of the fake-pearl phase. (It must be said: The quirky phase was also a reaction to a boyfriend who tended to date girls much quirkier than I.) There was nothing creative or affirming about my approach to dressing myself. It was just another way to try to fit into someone else's box.

I camouflaged myself in discount Ralph Lauren to prove that I could fit into a clique I never really wanted to join in the first place. I dyed my hair blue and stacked up quirky accessories in an attempt to prove, once and for all, that I was the master of my own appearance. The discount Ralph Lauren aligned me socially in a way I now regret; the ModCloth phase left me scratching at cheap polyester, teetering around town in an outfit that felt more clownish than cool. Both times, I experienced the squirmy, itchy sensation of wearing clothes that didn't quite fit.

That leaves me with the orange clogs. They were purchased during a brief obsession with clogs as a concept. To me, clogs were the hallmark of a self-assured woman—a clog bitch, if you will. Slip your feet into a pair of clogs, and you immediately become someone who owns a hand-crank apple corer and a tastefully eclectic record collection. Clogs send a *message*.

Clogs also hurt. They're not a comfortable shoe. I learned that the hard way after a single stroll in the orange clogs, purchased from a Scandinavian retailer during one of their rare sales. I left my house with a spring in my step—at least, as much of a spring as I could muster in a shoe designed to maim. A few blocks later, the clogs' rigid sides had torn horrible blisters into both of my feet. I hobbled back home, painting a gooey, bloody sunset across the orange leather tops. I grimaced my way up the stairs, stashed the shoes in the back of my closet, and slunk away to ice my wounds.

The orange clogs are still there, in the back of my closet, reminding me of what happens when I subject myself to discomfort in an attempt to prove a point. I couldn't return them after the blister goo incident, but I also can't bring myself to give them away. I'm stuck in clog limbo. I think it's because I still want to be the kind of person who wears them effortlessly. Ah, what I wouldn't give to pair them with some billowy-linen situation and walk for miles without a hint of foot chafe. The clogs represent a persona I want to inhabit.

The final frontier, if you will; the aspirational version of myself that I realistically know I'll never meet.

The clogs have the same effect as the preppy bows and the cowgirl cosplay and the Peter Pan collars. Every attempt at finding my style has been an exercise in trying on an unfamiliar skin. And every time, I've shed the skin after a few weeks, months, or years, which leaves me shivering, exposed, and occasionally blistered until the next aspirational persona comes along.

I've recently fallen back into the Comfort Years. Most of the time, I dress like a kid from *The Sandlot*, in oversized tees and fraying bike shorts and baseball caps. When I need to wear a little outfit, I opt for bright, primary colors and dresses that cover my butt with room to spare. I will, occasionally, wear a statement jumpsuit—but most of the time, I wear clothing that doesn't make any sort of statement at all. At this point, I know myself, and I'm not interested in slipping into an unfamiliar uniform for the someone else's benefit. Anyway, the only spaces I'm interested in occupying are the spaces that welcome a robust young woman who dresses like a camp counselor on leave.

And yet—*and yet*—the denim newsboy hat continues to haunt me. The world is clearly sprinting backward to the dog days of 2000s fashion, characterized by microminis and pubic mounds longing to break free. The stench of pleather fills the air, and our collective body mass index seems to be plummeting once again. (You might recall that Y2K fashion was hostile to anyone with a normal body. Low-rise pants didn't fit my ten-year-old body in 2004, and they don't fit my grown-up body now. I am moderately titted and moderately assed, and I require a standard zip-up fly, damn it.)

Like any trend, aughts fashion will come and go. Ed Hardy tank tops will sell for hundreds of dollars online; starlets will step out in barely-there sequined tops. The trend will pass me by just like it did the first time, leaving me pantsless and comfortable in my *Sanford and Son* T-shirt. Feel free to try the trends on for size; just proceed with caution. If you're unlucky enough to be photographed wearing a studded belt and a fuzzy purple cowboy hat, don't say I didn't warn you.

The Incredible Vibrating Teen

I hunched over the bathroom sink, peering at the green pill capsule held between my thumb and forefinger. It didn't look so bad. It was bigger than I'd have liked—smaller than a Baha Men HitClip, but large enough to form a noticeable lump in the back pocket of my bedazzled Buckle boot-cut jeans, which my mom had bought on the condition that I'd never wear them while eating, drinking, or scaling a chain-link fence. The capsule was smooth and shiny, seemingly slick enough to slither past my esophagus with minimal trauma. I glanced up at myself in the mirror and blinked my eyes three times, hard. That wasn't enough, so I blinked them three more times. *"Not enough!"* screeched my relentless prefrontal cortex, so I blinked two more times, jerked my neck hard to the left, and clenched my right big toe for five seconds. Temporarily satisfied, my prefrontal cortex gave its approval: *"Go ahead."*

I popped the pill into my mouth, chased it with a mouthful of water from a waxy Dixie rinse cup, and tried to swallow. The pill bounced off my tensed tongue and clanged against the back of my throat, Liberty Bell–style, forcing me to upchuck the mouthful of water and the pill into the sink with a hearty *CACK*. I steeled myself for another go, pausing momentarily to raise my eyebrows skyward for roughly thirty seconds until they felt *correct*. This time, I placed the pill all the way on the back of my tongue before reaching for the Dixie cup. But the pill rolled into the center of my gag zone, and I *CACK*ed it up along with the remnants of a saltine cracker stored in my permanent retainer. *"Idiot!"* cackled my prefrontal cortex. *"You're fifteen years old, and you can't swallow pills! Now, twirl your fingers over and over again for six minutes or your parents will die."*

I had mostly gotten away with the pill aversion until this moment. I relied on bubble gum–flavored amoxicillin syrup to cure my annual bouts of strep throat and skipped ibuprofen in favor of sickly-sweet liquid Motrin for period cramps. But there are very few drugs to help teens control their compulsive motor tics, and none of them come in sour gummy form. I was left with two choices: learn to swallow the pills, or continue navigating my fraught teen years with my very visible condition, which had been misdiagnosed by a stern pediatric neurologist earlier that day.

"It's Tourette's," the pediatric neurologist sighed as I hunched awkwardly over a plastic table covered with sensory toys. It wasn't Tourette's, but the doctor clearly hated teens and wanted me out of his office so he could focus on prescribing antipsychotics to hyperactive six-year-olds. He made his diagnosis entirely based on my motor tics—rolling and blinking my eyes, wiggling my nose from side to side, tormenting myself with a complex series of finger and toe movements. If he had taken the time to examine me carefully, he'd have noticed the giant blinking sign across my forehead that spelled out OBSESSIVE-COMPULSIVE DISORDER. For one thing, my tics weren't consistent with a Tourette's diagnosis. Most Tourette's cases peak around the age of ten; my tics peaked midway through high school, just as I was learning to grind to the Ying Yang Twins. I also didn't have any vocal tics, save the occasional bout of obsessive throat-clearing, which was fueled not by a neurological urge but by a fear of spontaneous anaphylactic shock. (*If I can clear my throat, it's probably not swelling shut*, I thought as I coughed out a series of rhythmic *ahems* to the cadence of "Groove Is in the Heart.")

Most importantly, my tics coincided with a crushing list of fears, rituals, and intrusive imaginings that ranged from stabbing my beloved pet with a knitting needle to leaping up in biology class to gyrate into my hot teacher's crotch. My OCD was textbook; still, the neurologist was a busy man. He took one look at my twitching shoulders, adjusted his framed diploma, and sent me tumbling out of his office with a lazy diagnosis and a one-way ticket to Pharmaceutical Nation.

This left me with the pills. I'm not sure why I had such a hard time swallowing pills, though I'm sure it had something to do with my intensifying catastrophic thoughts. What if I tried to swallow a pill and it slid into my lung, burying itself in a lymph node? What if I was allergic to the pill casing—not the medicine, the *casing*—and my throat swelled shut before anyone knew what was wrong with me? (Cue another frantic series of rhythmic *ahems* to the cadence of Pitbull's "Hotel Room Service.") What if I choked on the pill in a public setting and my crush had to stick his finger down my throat, causing me to blow chunks all over his Weird Al messenger bag? I'd be forced to drop out of school.

Any of those possibilities were better than the situation at hand. On good days, I twitched gently. On bad days, my tics send me herky-jerking around like a cartoon cat electrocuted on a lightning rod. My body never felt *right*, and I spent every waking minute contorting it in freaky directions to satisfy my shrewish prefrontal cortex. Neck to the left. Harder. Shoulder blade jerked to the right, then tensed for twelve seconds. *Harder.*

Tics aren't like other OCD symptoms. They're not rituals, per se; they're more like a physical manifestation of one's obsessions. Think of the most horrible itch you can imagine; now, imagine being compelled to scratch it over and over again until it hurts. Why? I have no idea, and I certainly didn't receive any insight from the doctor. All I knew was that the tics got worse when I felt anxious, which was always. They peaked at bedtime and kept me up for hours, resulting in corpselike under-eye circles and the kind of exhaustion that left me snoring during Mrs. Dickey's extra-credit screening of *The Motorcycle Diaries*. That was the true tragedy—not the physical pain and fatigue I felt from flailing nonstop, but the fact that I was too distracted to absorb Che Guevara's sex appeal into my humid pubescent aura.

At first, the tics were easy to hide. A finger twirl here; a nose twitch there. For a while, I was able to disguise the latter as a quirky nod to 1960s pop culture. "*Bewitched*!" cried my gleeful drama teacher as I wiggled my nose covertly. I glanced up. "What?" I asked, holding my hand over my nose to conceal another wiggle. "You're doing *Bewitched*! Like Elizabeth Montgomery! So cute!" she crowed. "Uh, yeah," I stuttered, totally clueless. "I love *Bewitched*."

But left untreated, my OCD turned into ultrasticky fly paper, snagging everything in my path and turning everyday movements into mandatory tic sequences that must be repeated *just so*. I'd lean down to pick a pencil up off the floor, slightly extending my neck in the process. My brain would then latch on to that slight neck extension, forcing me to repeat the movement until I felt *right* again. I'd twirl my pinky finger a certain way while tying my shoe; I'd then feel compelled to twirl it again and again in the exact same way until my joints click-clacked like Japanese beetles. Think of my brain's tic sector as a lazy torturer. Instead of devising twisted torture methods, the torturer simply waits for the torturee to contort themselves into some uncomfortable position. "Did that suck?" the torturer asks. "Yes? Great. Do it again and again and again."

Some of the tics were short-lived, minor compulsions satisfied within a matter of hours or days. But some produced such a rich sensation that they've stayed with me to this day, like the shoulder-rolling tic that I developed after a swim team group stretch session. The shoulder roll still plagues me, cropping up a few times an hour on a good day. I can remember exactly how it started. My team-mates and I were warming up with arm circles, and I rotated my right shoulder blade sharply behind me and tensed my neck to lean into the stretch.

My prefrontal cortex went nuts. "*YES, GOD, YES*," my brain screamed—so I repeated the movement. "*NO, NOT LIKE THAT*," my brain screamed, so I repeated the movement harder and faster until it felt *right*. I felt relief, but only for a moment.

The shoulder roll is my most visible tic to date. Unlike my charming nose wiggle, the shoulder roll was a sweeping motion, often accompanied by the *pop-pop-pop* of my tight back muscles. "Um, Lillian?" Lauren Veldez whispered one day, leaning forward midway through a sophomore biology lecture. "Are you okay? Something insane is happening with your back." I spun around and looked her dead in the eye. "I *HAVE* a *CONDITION*," I sniffed. I then asked to go to the bathroom so I could spend five minutes shimmying my shoulders in peace.

Lauren wasn't the only classmate to notice my near-constant writhing. The tics threatened my budding performance career as a passionate, though only passably talented, member of my school's drama club and debate team. Can you imagine staying in character as a citizen of Nool in *Seussical the Musical* when you can't stop blinking? Can you *fathom* the *horror* of compulsive finger-twirling and neck-jerking during an extemporaneous speaking event at a debate tournament in Neosho, Missouri? Yelling at your peers about Julian Assange is humiliating enough without the added burden of obsessive lip-licking.

Though the tics were, and are, physically uncomfortable, their sheer visibility was what landed me in the neurologist's office. I remember riding home from a debate tournament in the passenger seat of my dad's sedan, weeping into my hands as I kicked off my tasteful JCPenney pumps. A judge had remarked that my nose-twitching was "distracting" and knocked me a point on my scoring sheet, recommending that I practice my speaking skills in the mirror.

"*NO ONE* knows how this feels," I sobbed in supreme teenager fashion. "Everyone is *STARING AT ME*." My dad told me to buck up, at which point I shrilly yelled out my plans to get a huge tattoo that spelled out "**I am not my affliction**" in thick medieval script the moment I turned eighteen.

"You are not afflicted," my dad groaned, shaking his head as I stamped my feet into the dashboard. He reminded me that it could be much worse—I could have motor tics and a really huge mole.

Weeks after my neurological misdiagnosis, I still couldn't swallow the pills. I tried sticking my tongue out like a Juggalo and squeezing my eyes shut; I tried staring at myself in the mirror and hyping myself up, *Remember the Titans*–style. Nothing worked. I was afflicted for life, it seemed. I pictured myself at eighty, twitching my way into a nursing home somehow already populated with my snottiest high school classmates. The thought made me despondent; the despondency made me depressed. I was physically sore from the tics, tired from the lack of sleep, and scared of my own teenage emotions.

My desperation was such that I resorted to truly craven behavior: sprinkling the contents of my pill capsules over my daily PB&J sandwich. In my mind, this was convenient, as I was supposed to take the pills with lunch. I emptied the capsules into a small plastic bag before school and packed the bag in my lunchbox. This accomplished two things: First, it ensured that I'd be able to consume the pills' contents without actually swallowing the pills; second, it made it look like I was packing crank in my insulated lunch box, which was really cool.

Earlier that year, a boy with two first names and flippy bangs got caught smuggling a thermos full of booze into Mrs. Bruce's English class. It's not like he was subtle about it. "Wanna know what's in this thermos?" he asked, eyebrows wiggling. He cracked it open.

"Pure vodka. Stolich-NAYA, baby," he said, taking an impish swig. Mrs. Bruce walked into the room ready to bust him, but it didn't matter. He had cemented himself in Cool Dude history alongside the kid who ordered a pizza to geometry class and the girl who flashed nipple at the back-to-school dance. I wanted a piece of that glory.

I made a huge show of extracting the bag of mysterious powder from my lunch box and dumping it onto my peanut butter sandwich. Pete Langston looked pointedly at the powder. "What is *that*?" he asked, arms folded. I shot him a wild look. "Pete, this is CRACK," I declared, unclear on the physical properties of actual crack cocaine. Pete said nothing, and I took a huge bite of the sandwich. I quickly realized that the powder inside pill capsules is the worst-tasting thing on earth. I gagged, sputtered, chucked the sandwich into the trash, and sprinted to the vending machine to purchase a bag of Salsitas to hold me over until after school.

Obsessive-compulsive disorder is not high-octane perfec-tionism, despite what some smugly organized folk may tell you. All Container Store Rewards Club members are perfectionists, but only a handful of them are bona fide OCD cases. I'm both, but I don't think either trait has anything to do with the other. Yes, I arrange my dry goods in stackable jars and plan my meals using color-coded spreadsheets, but I don't do those things because I *must*—I do them because I want to. Meanwhile, I twitch my shoulders and jerk my neck because I *must*, even though I really, really don't want to. My tidy preferences are not the result of compulsion; I could, ostensibly, leave my spice jars unalphabetized without feeling a wave of red-hot panic. It'd be annoying, and it might even make me anxious, but I am ultimately the master of my spice jars.

While I may be the master of my spice jars, I am most definitely not the master of my body. I cannot, and probably never will, resist the pull to complete my tic sequences. I can hold them off for a bit, gritting my teeth as I fight against the urge to correct myself. But eventually, I must twitch the shoulder. I must twirl the fingers. I must tense the calf muscle until it cramps and sends me flopping in pain like a halibut out of water. My limbs hang on fine-spun threads; at any moment, my misfiring puppet master of a brain can jerk me around. Sometimes, I think about what would happen if I became paralyzed from the neck down. Would my body still find a way to carry out the tics? Or would I lose my mind completely, burning alive with the agony of unrequited compulsion?

The pills corrected none of this, even after I learned to choke them down. The neurologist started by prescribing me risperidone, an antipsychotic used to control tics in Tourette's patients. Risperidone's side effects are numerous and fearsome, ranging from muscle stiffness and confusion to uncontrollable facial movements and painful, long-lasting erections. I experienced neither erection nor tic relief. Instead, I grew angry and taciturn, unable to pay attention in class or control the mood swings that already racked my teenage brain. After a few months of living with Beelzebub herself, my parents took me off the risperidone and switched me to a milder cocktail: Zoloft (the doctor reasoned it would chill me out, thus calming my tics) and Topamax, an anti-epileptic drug affectionately called "Dopamax" for its head-fuzzying effects. The combination quieted my tics, but it also flatlined my energy levels in a way that made it impossible to navigate the already-labyrinthine rules of teenage engagement.

I thought I was used to fatigue after the tics kept me up night after night, but that was nothing compared to the bone-deep exhaustion I felt on the drugs. I began to lose entire stretches of time. I'd blink and be unable to account for the last two hours, though my body had somehow found its way from one point to another. It was all I could do to make it to 2:55 p.m., when I'd creep bleary-eyed into the passenger seat of my mom's SUV, drift off with my cheek against the cool window, then crawl into bed to nap until dinnertime.

This left no time for homework; worse, it left no time for my revolving door of cretin boyfriends. I excelled at attracting them during the day, prying my bloodshot eyes open as I pranced from class to class. But come late afternoon, my meager energy supply ran out and left me crumpled corpselike on the floor, bereft of personality and unable to do anything but stare at the ceiling. I found myself weeping quietly as Adam Koonce looked at the floor and ended our two-month relationship in search of someone "more on my level, energy-wise." I couldn't blame him. Every time I executed my sparkling performance of a daytime personality, it was to disguise the fact that my brain was a black, velvety expanse suited only for the deep sleep of the pharmaceutically compromised.

In some ways, my catatonia was lush. I drifted between sleeps, eyes unfocused and fists softly clenching and unclenching. It certainly blunted the Pythagorean torment of Mrs. Franklin's trigonometry class. But I, a lifelong teacher's pet, suddenly couldn't retain the most basic academic principles. This was a problem at my fiercely competitive high school, where the prom king sported a rolling backpack and early admission to Caltech.

My chemically induced despondency also went directly against my life's mission: to be everything to everyone, all the time. The tics peaked along with the need to ensure that I was equally palatable to family members, friends, boyfriends, and teachers. The pills made me too sleepy for any of that, which worried me. If I couldn't organize food drives and star in school plays and lead the swim team to victory and direct the Student Council with the fervor of a military mastermind, why try at anything? If I didn't have the energy to commandeer the school PA system and deliver the afternoon announcements with the zeal of a Branson auctioneer, what was the point?

My only hope was using my scant bursts of energy to fake it—first, by charming my teachers and convincing them to give me extra time on assignments; second, by dipping my toe into every single social circle in what may be modern history's most ambitious performance of adolescent normalcy. The proof's in my high school yearbook. Flip to the back and you'll find black-and-white photos of every student organization, smiling members all arranged by height. I'm in most of these photos. On one page, I'm peeking sheepishly out of a crowd of Key Club members. On the next page, I'm leaning against two of my fellow Peer Mediators, arms crossed in a show of grand solidarity. Keep flipping and you'll see me among the Drama Club, the Debate Team, the Student Council, and a small coalition of students dedicated to internet neutrality. In all these photos, I'm smiling eagerly among my peers, standing somewhere near the middle in a worn-out crewneck sweatshirt. But look closely and you'll see that I'm pulled taut. There's a harsh smile stretched across my face, and my eyebrows are raised frantically in a way that causes deep ridges to form across my forehead. It's the face of someone who is too tired to stand up, but still feels compelled to perform excellence in every way possible.

Eventually, I figured out my dosage. After college, a savvy psychiatrist took one look at me and scoffed at my Tourette's diagnosis, weaning me off both the Zoloft and the Topamax and replacing them with a single anti-anxiety drug that did more for my *affliction* than any of the drugs that had slithered through my veins throughout adolescence. I still can't account for the large swaths of time I lost to those drugs. It's as though some government worker has gone through and redacted sections of my teenage memories, replacing them with inky black spots I'll never be able to clear. I'm left with vague high school–shaped memories. Even without the benefit of mind-addling pharmaceuticals, most adults look back on their adolescence with a deep, guttural cringe. I look back on mine with a level of distrust typically reserved for alcoholic brownouts.

I remember some things. I remember driving to a nearby farm town for a football game and running over an opossum in my Nissan Maxima. I couldn't stand to leave it wriggling on the asphalt, so I stopped the car with a lurch and backed over it, then drove away with a bloodcurdling, squicked-out scream. I remember the smell of the Drama Club costume closet, where I very nearly slapped a bossy girl named after an apple. I remember rolling up my sweatshirt, painting my stomach for a football game, and spending the first quarter clenching my abs so tightly that I got lightheaded and had to leave early. I remember the mother of one particular paramour; she accused me of having a menstrual disorder after I yelled at her pervert son. I remember eating waffles with my best friend on the morning of graduation, nervously stacking Smuckers jelly packets and worrying about what came next.

Everything else is anyone's guess. I might as well have spent four years in a blindfold, stumbling down my high school's stairwells and interacting with other clumsy teens in total darkness. I hope I was generally agreeable, though there's a good chance that the pills addled me beyond the point of sociability.

Where I once saw my tics as an affliction, I now see them as mostly an annoyance. This isn't a tale of radical self-acceptance; my tics are often frustrating, sometimes painful, and generally inconvenient. If I were a healthier, more productive person, I'd take this moment to reflect on what my tics have taught me. If I were a TikToker, I'd cast myself as some sort of neurodivergent superhero. "My tics might be annoying sometimes," I'd say, latching on to a deeply unflattering viral dance. "But I wouldn't want it any other way."

I am neither a productive person nor a TikToker, nor am I especially comfortable with the neurodivergent label. Where does that leave me? Existing in ambiguity, I guess. I'll have to find peace in the fact that most of my adolescence is hidden under an inkblot. I suppose I could go trawling through social media, looking for archaeological clues as to my behavior in 2009. Honestly, I'd rather not dredge up years' worth of cringe-inducing "rawr xD" wall postings. Maybe my bad memory is a good thing. Maybe it's a protective measure to keep me from dwelling on the general humiliation of the late aughts. Maybe it's an attempt to pull myself up by my pharmaceutically lubricated bootstraps and dismiss the very real pain of a neurological diagnosis at fifteen.

Most likely, it's an ongoing exercise in manufactured peace, in leaning into the discomfort of not knowing. More than once, I've assured myself that my high school classmates were far too busy picking PB&J crumbs out of their teeth to pay attention to my odd flailing. I repeat the mantra of self-conscious women everywhere: *Everyone is too focused on their own weirdness to worry about yours. No one remembers your embarrassing moments.* Then I remember the time a classmate broke his leg during a faculty basketball game. The school nurse hauled him away, weeping in a wheelchair. The student body broke into spontaneous applause. The vice principal screamed into a bullhorn: "GO BULLDOGS!" I will remember that day until the sun dies.

It stands to reason, then, that someone remembers my own high school strangeness. Maybe former classmates remember me as pharmaceutically compromised; maybe they just remember me as annoying. Maybe I've frightened a stranger on an airplane, seated three rows behind me with a perfect view of my herky-jerky shoulder. Maybe I've frightened a stranger on an airplane for a reason entirely unrelated to my perennial flailing. Maybe I should just shut up and take my pills.

Beware the Howler

I was raised in the shadow of a Yakov Smirnoff billboard. It's on State Highway 248, a half hour from my parents' place near the Missouri–Arkansas border. Glance up and you'll see the Ukrainian comic's grinning face, thirty feet in the air and partially camouflaged by a Cossack fur hat. Below him lies a stick of dynamite. DANGER! the billboard reads. EXPLOSIVE LAUGHTER! WITH YAKOV.

Drive a few miles down the highway and you'll find Yakov's two-thousand-seat Branson comedy theater. Drive a few miles in the other direction and you'll find my hometown. Springfield is the third-largest city in Missouri, with a population that recently broke 160,000 and a shiny new Costco to prove it. It's half the size of St. Louis, the next-largest city. You can drive from one end of town to the other in about twenty minutes if you're really cooking, though no one ever is.

Like the Yakov billboard, Springfield is weird. In a good way, mostly. I've always rolled my eyes at the rhetoric surrounding other "weird" towns—places like Austin, Texas, or Portland, Oregon. Sure, your city might have a robust penny-farthing racing community, but Springfield has miles of underground limestone tunnels in which the United States government stores 1.4 billion pounds of cheese. Brag about your hometown heroes all you want; Springfield has the Baldknobbers, a group of fearsome masked vigilantes who stalked outlaws and corrupt government officials throughout the nineteenth century. Oh, your town square's the site of an infamous Revolutionary War skirmish? Great. Mine's the site of the nation's first one-on-one quick-draw duel, which took place in 1865 between Wild Bill Hickok and Davis K. Tutt. Legend has it that the shoot-out began as an argument over a gambling debt, prompting Tutt to seize Wild Bill's prized watch as collateral. Humiliated, Wild Bill challenged Tutt to a duel and killed him on the spot. After a three-day trial, a jury acquitted Wild Bill of manslaughter. They decided he had a pretty good reason for offing Tutt. A gentleman must accessorize.

Like I said, Springfield's weird. I once heard someone describe the area as a "freaky vortex," a bubbling cauldron that spits out the strangest artifacts—artifacts like Brad Pitt, who went to high school with my mother. He still comes home for the holidays, treating vigilant locals to selfies at an upscale pizza joint. When he's not around, we settle for his brother, who is unironically named Doug Pitt.

And while the latest census data puts the median income around $38,000, it's hard to classify Springfield as a blue-collar town. It's got the quirk of a college town and the sprawl of a farming community; a Marxist bookstore, a firearms dealer, and a Route 66 museum are all located within a one-mile radius of the town square. There's an emo ice cream parlor that serves charcoal-dyed soft-serve; there's a weekly bluegrass hour on the local NPR station. Close your eyes and throw a Yakov flyer and you might hit a grizzled moonshiner, but you're just as likely to hit the frontman of a moderately successful indie rock band. Accents run the gamut from deep, twangy hill chatter to vocally fried barista-speak. We've got open-carrying millionaires who made their fortunes in the trailer hitch industry;

we've got crunchy California transplants eager to shake up the composting scene. For every berry farm, there's a semirural gated McMansion complex; for every McMansion, there's a cozy midcentury bungalow flanked by Little Free Libraries. It's a place full of contradictions. A place full of lore.

It makes sense that urban legends would flourish in a contradictory town like Springfield. The topography alone is pretty spooky. The Ozark Mountains ooze hillbilly folklore, with swirling mists that produce claims of howling beasts and vigilantes in black horned hoods. Down below, untouched caves lie beneath ancient layers of dolomite. In between, urban legends are born of conflicting accounts. There's the abandoned plot of land near my childhood home that supposedly once housed Camp Winoka, an apocryphal summer camp where a dozen Girl Scouts were brutally slaughtered. Some say there never was a camp there; others say it was Cubs, not Girl Scouts. Once, my sister went to see for herself. She swears she saw members of a devil-worshipping cult through the trees. Her friends say it was a sorority.

Then there's the Albino Farm, an overgrown nineteenth-century settlement on Springfield's far north side. It's allegedly haunted by the ghost of a spiteful groundskeeper with albinism. Or did the groundskeeper's wife have albinism? Or did the groundskeeper simply breed albino catfish? And are we even still using *albino* as a descriptor? Or *groundskeeper*?

My favorite legend involves a beast that can't make up its mind. Growing up, I kept my eyes peeled for the Ozark Howler, also known as the Hoo-Hoo, the Nightshade Bear, or the Devil Cat. The Howler is said to stalk the Ozark Mountains' dark, craggy ridges, guarding the no-man's-land near the Missouri–Arkansas border. The beast is bear-sized with stocky legs, black shaggy hair, glowing red eyes, and thick, horrible horns. Even worse is the Howler's telltale cry, described as something between a wolf's howl, an elk's bugle, and the laugh of a hyena.

Everybody's Favorite

I learned about the Howler in a library book. I was nine or ten, and I had already plowed through my elementary school's kiddie horror section, stealing away with five *Bunnicula* paperbacks at a time. I was hard on library books, baptizing *Scary Stories to Tell in the Dark* anthologies in the bathtub until I emerged, shriveled and shivering, to read under the covers. I broke spines and dog-eared pages with abandon until the Dewey Decimaled horror section seemed to beg for respite. At that point, I moved on to the local history shelf. I pawed through pamphlets for nearby Civil War battlefields and impatiently sampled an 1880 homesteader's diary. Finally, I landed on a well-worn collection of Ozarks myths and legends. I lowered myself to the ground, sitting cross-legged on the thick carpet as I took in tales of a beast that's part cat, part bear, and part wolf.

No one can agree on the Howler's exact physical characteristics. The only thing we *can* agree on is that it'll just as soon eat you as look at you. That's what makes it so scary—by the time you realize what you're looking at, it's too late. The Howler contains menacing multitudes, capable of shifting into everyone's worst nightmare. One minute, it's a dusty old dog curled up by the fire; the next, it's eating your granny. It's lupine to some and ursine to others. It is unwieldy, dodging capture and definition, beholden to no one and mastered only by otherworldly possibility. It's the perfect cryptid for a town like Springfield, which can't seem to make up its mind about what kind of town it wants to be. And it's the perfect cryptid for me, a breathlessly nostalgic Ozarks expat who can't make up my mind about my relationship with my hometown.

I didn't leave Missouri until I was twenty-four, later than most. My hometown is one of those places where you either scuttle away at eighteen or stay for life, sucked in by affordable real estate and, if you're lucky, a wild sexual affair with a smoothie artist at the local health food store. I stuck around for a cheap college education, got a few jobs under my belt, and then headed north to Chicago to live out my big-city fantasy. The fantasy had been brewing since I first visited Chicago at twenty and wept in awe upon seeing a two-story Walgreens, *with* escalator. Other than the giant Walgreens, I didn't have a great reason for choosing Chicago, though I now know it to be the greatest city in the world. There are lots of cities, and probably lots of multistory Walgreens pharmacies. In the end, Chicago was the biggest city within U-Hauling distance at a time when I felt restlessly, frantically itchy.

I've always been itchy, though not in the way you'd expect from syrupy Hallmark depictions of small-town girls longing to break free. I was—still am—a homebody. I didn't feel oppressed by my surroundings; I felt oppressed by my own uncertainty. I spent my teen years scratching at that sense of oppressive possibility; the knowledge that the world could, someday, be mine for the taking, if I only had the courage to leave my parents' driveway. I mean that literally: I used to spend warm nights leaning against the garage door, staring upward in the most dramatic possible interpretation of teen angst and feeling like I was about to bust out of my skin amid the vastness of rural suburbia.

The angst lay entirely in my own terror of growing up, of shape-shifting into something that my hometown might find as horrific as the Howler. I wanted to become something large and loud, something fanged and famous, the kind of person who lives in a sleek high-rise and smokes from a long-handled jade cigarette holder and leaves her hometown without looking back. At the same time, I wanted to curl up under my great-grandmother's scratchy crocheted afghan and renovate the farmhouse a mile from my parents' place, becoming the kind of person who smells of bonfires and develops a deeper, richer twang with age. I felt those menacing multitudes brewing deep in my pseudo-hillbilly heart, and I was terrified. I didn't want to let anyone down. In the end, the only way to treat the itch was to make a move, to slink away from the prying eyes of the Ozarks and figure out what I wanted on my own terms.

My family made it hard to move away. Most of them live within a ten-mile radius, and I struggle with an advanced case of paranoid FOMO, prone to teary-eyed brattiness when anyone has fun without me. My family is also full of poor communicators. My siblings and I do okay, mostly swapping hideous selfies and diarrheal anecdotes. My parents are worse. My dad and I communicate almost exclusively via screenshots of old *Far Side* strips; not long ago, my mom mailed me a greeting card:

Thinking of you. I hope we get to live near each other again before I die.

FOMO and sporadic texting aside, my family is rich with superstition and exaggeration. They're not the kind of people you want to offend by moving far away. My mother's people trickled out of hills and hollers, starting pig farms and doing hair and getting married and divorced enough times to produce me, a confused girl child with strong legs and a weak constitution. We've never been good record-keepers, with elders too dazed from cigarette smoke to pass along accurate anecdotes. My mother tells me how her father ran wild with his brother Randy, seducing unsuspecting women with dirty music and devilish good looks. My aunt tells me my grandmother once saved a kid's life by diving ten feet into the deep end of a public pool with her shoes on. My great-uncle tells me that somebody, at some point, shot and ate a squirrel.

My father's side of the family is less exciting, though it doesn't stop him from self-mythologizing. He's a transplant from Texas who employs his lingering Amarillo accent to insist that Houston is not, in fact, *real* Texas. He brags about eating canned rattlesnake. He insists that he once saw Stevie Nicks naked. He's the only person I know who lacks a healthy fear of funnel clouds, which is a problem because my hometown is situated in the heart of Tornado Alley. Once, he piled my siblings and me into the backseat during a tornado warning, bone-chilling sirens and all, to do a little grocery shopping. After our cart was full, the store manager came over the loudspeaker to announce that a mean twister had touched down nearby. My dad took this as a challenge, calmly placed us back in the truck with the groceries, and zipped home down the highway, racing the black cloud as it got bigger and bigger behind us. *This is how I die*, I thought. *In a car with my stupid, round-headed kid brother.*

So, yes, things get blown out of proportion in my family. I'm the child of a father who laughs in the face of funnel clouds and a mother who knows how to use lit cigarettes to extract ticks from her flesh. With those roots, it's no wonder I lapped up local mythology and leaned into the golden rule of mythmaking: that the scariest bits exist in the empty spaces. The glint in a werewolf's yellow eye; the smell of sulfur before a demon descends on an unsuspecting village; the sound of a hook screeching against the hood of a parked car. As I prepared to leave Missouri, I knew it was time to fill my own empty spaces, potentially creating something beastly in the process. I felt like a werewolf—hiding from prying eyes, not wanting anyone to see me transform.

I was kidding myself; the transformation had already begun. I spent my early twenties growing resentful of my surroundings. I had seen one too many bruise-colored tornado skies and endured one too many catcalls from cruel young men in pickup trucks. I had undergone a full-scale sociopolitical awakening that didn't square with my parents' allegiance to Mark Levin. I had become hypersensitive to the ugly parts of home, rolling my eyes at the rotting hay bales spray-painted with alt-right messaging and avoiding my favorite coffee shops, which suddenly seemed to be crawling with sneaky Evangelicals disguised beneath cool beanies. One minute, they're serving you an expertly crafted cortado or advising you on Mailchimp strategy; the next, they're sadly shaking their heads at your sexuality. They wear hipness as a skin, lacing up their lightly worn Doc Martens and strutting into Sunday morning service to remind themselves of their own noxious superiority. They're the Roger Chillingworths of the Soylent age.

As I considered the beastly aspects of home, I began to feel scrutinized in a way I couldn't stand. In a town like mine, anonymity is sacrificed in favor of cheap gas. Everyone knows everyone's business, and my business had grown progressively messier as I entered adulthood. I could walk through the town square and see my old Sunday school teacher, a man who'd once drunkenly tried to run me over on his longboard, and five people who all knew the intimate details of my latest breakup. It made me feel like I was thirteen again, sitting in my parents' driveway and wriggling around in too-tight skin. It made me bitter. It made me crass and lazy, joining outsiders in treating the Ozarks as a punch line. I rolled my eyes at the folklore I used to love and laughed along with yee-yee memes about the merits of the humble corncob as a toileting implement. The hills had lost their luster; my hometown had transformed into an entirely unknown beast. I had, too.

So I moved. I rented an apartment and settled into Chicago's far north side, all feminist bookstores and vintage markets and coffee shops that almost never set off my Evangelical radar. I relished the anonymity, astonished that I could strut braless down the sidewalk without garnering the disapproval of a former employer. I could live there for years, I reasoned, and never run into anyone from junior high.

I was shocked the first time I got catcalled by a man in a pickup truck. I was walking down my Chicago neighborhood's charming main street, window-shopping and swinging my winsome tote bag. I heard him—"NICE ASS!"—before I saw him. I whirled around and stared at him in disbelief. "YOU CAN'T DO THAT HERE!" I yelled after him, shaking my fist. "DON'T YOU KNOW THIS IS A BLUE STATE???!!!"

Not long after, I started noticing cracks in my glamorously imagined big-city facade. The catcalls continued. Local political leaders outed themselves as bigots. One of my neighbors debuted a bumper sticker that read I'M PROUD TO BE AN AMERICAN. IF YOU'RE NOT—PISS OFF!

Naive and self-satisfied, I thought I had left such sentiments behind in the land of Yakov Smirnoff billboards. Turns out, that stuff lives everywhere. Some places are just better at hiding it.

I started missing home about a month into my lease. My hometown bitterness had emboldened me, bolstering my courage and sending me north. The scorn faded almost immediately after I moved. I became ardently defensive of the Ozarks, rearing back with a roar every time someone dared perpetuate tired hillbilly stereotypes. I rolled my eyes at the coworker who asked if I'd ever eaten a possum. (No—they're very hard to catch.) I snarled at peers who suggested that Ozarks politicians are an effective measure of locals' values, as if the region hasn't been held hostage by high-powered bigots for generations. Once, on a trip home, I snapped at a gaggle of travelers waiting in line at the Springfield-Branson National Airport coffee shop. They were debating their plan of action during a long layover. "We might as well stay put," sniffed one woman in a pair of bejeweled riding boots. "It's not as though there's anything around here other than cow patties." I shot her a look liable to kill Wild Bill Hickok himself.

I still miss the Ozarks. I miss the Uranus Fudge Factory on Interstate 44. I miss the Sucker Days fish festival. I miss hillbilly music on AM radio. I miss Silver Dollar City, the 1880s theme park that is home to America's fastest wooden roller coaster. Strangely, I even miss the Yakov billboards en route to Branson, a spiritual destination unlike any other. There, fifty-six dollars will get you a ticket to *JESUS!*, a two-hour Christian stage production starring a white guy in the titular role. After that, you can follow the scent of righteous fraud down Highway 86 to visit televangelist Jim Bakker. When he's not preaching, Bakker sells a variety of wares in preparation for the End of Days, including prophetic texts like *Prosperity and the Coming Apocalypse* and a $450 bucket containing enough buttermilk pancake mix to sustain a family of five through the downfall of man.

Only in Branson is the life of Christ retold in a pyrotechnic frenzy. Only in Branson can you drink warm Sprite out of a plastic cowboy boot while a thirty-foot holographic Dolly Parton sings the national anthem. Only in Branson can you scarf down a funnel cake, puke on a log flume ride, and fall asleep in a happy stupor as a traveling family bluegrass band sings of sorrow.

My relationship with Branson rests mostly on nostalgia; my relationship with my hometown, complicated though it may be, rests on a stronger foundation. You can critique a thing and still love it, I think. Anyone who knows me knows that my criticism is marbled with affection. There are good, good things in the Ozarks. There's the burgeoning mutual aid network dedicated to making life easier for the residents the state wants to forget. There's the rolling hills and the nighttime quiet that I once found so suffocating. There's a pretty thirty-acre hayfield up the road from my parents' place. There's the cohort of friends who grew up and stayed put.

And there's me, left with a complicated attachment to this wildly contradictory place that feels somehow suspended in Jell-O. I go back and back and back to the fiendish mountains of my childhood, wanting them to be proud of me, but knowing that I've grown into something they maybe wouldn't like. Politically speaking, I'm a huge disappointment. I'm almost thirty and I am unmarried, unfertilized, and heavily tattooed. I read dirty books and fancy myself a socialist and drive a slime-colored hatchback. I'm comfortable with the person I've become, but I often worry that the hills won't love me anymore. This is irrational. The hills don't care what I do.

What worries me more is disappointing the people who inhabit those hills. I'm more outspoken since moving, a fact that leads my family and I into knock-down, drag-out screaming matches. I'm still hurt by our political differences, which feel a lot more personal than they used to. And while it's painful to know that I can't shape my parents in the ways I want, it's illuminating to see their unsavory bits clearly and love their interiority all the same. I've watched my people take all manner of different shapes, sprouting horns and spitting venom and then shrinking back down to the size of a pet rabbit to nuzzle my shoulder. This is what it means to be a family: to love, horns and all.

I go back home to the hills a few times a year to hug my parents and stuff myself full to bursting with my favorite frozen custard. It's a long drive, so I stay the week. While I'm there, I make a point to drive up into the hills and remember what quiet sounds like. I'll head for the rocky, well-trodden trails along the banks of the James River, and I'll do my best to ignore the blown-up photo of a gooey fetus on the anti-abortion billboard down Highway 60. I'll park on the side of the road and trek into the woods, swatting spiderwebs out of my eyes and listening to the crunch of the gravel beneath me. If I'm lucky, I'll have the trail to myself. I'll listen for the spaces in between my own breathing, embarrassingly ragged as I scale a steep switchback. I'll listen beyond my own footsteps, peering soundlessly into a clearing deep in the woods. Then, in that quiet, I'll hear a beast cry out in a way that sounds a bit like a wolf's howl, an elk's bugle, the cackle of a hyena. No one knows exactly what the Howler sounds like—but I'll know it when I hear it.

I stopped being afraid of the Ozark Howler years ago. I think I understand the beast now. Hell, some days I *am* the beast. Like the Howler, I've morphed into countless different shapes. I've threatened passersby with my gnarled horns; I've reared up and presented a pair of razor-sharp cloven hooves. I've shed my skin and slithered into small spaces, afraid to make myself known. I've felt alone and misunderstood in the hills of my birth, but I've also relished in the impossibility of their limestone labyrinths and unknowable, incorrigible residents.

Sometimes I still feel that lump in my throat when I can't picture my own final form. I can't slot my grown-up self into an identity designed to please my family. Even now, I can't make up my mind. Do I want more space or less? Do I want to live in quiet or an inescapable Technicolor din? How do I choose with the knowledge that I'll be misunderstood either way—that some might see me reworking myself and assume I'm vying for the destruction of the place that first held me? Even now, I get itchy knowing that I may never be finished, and that I'll keep shifting and slinking through the trees, Howler-like.

My hometown will never shape-shift into a less complicated beast. I'll never be able to contort myself into the shape of a perfect daughter. Instead, I'll do my best to honor the legend. I'll keep waxing poetic about Missouri's hollers to anyone who'll listen. I'll keep making the day-long trip home for a bite of frozen custard. Occasionally, I'll sleep with the lights on, sitting up in bed with teeth a-chatter for fear of the beast that lurks in the shadows—but most of the time, I'll live with it. I'll scratch the Howler behind the ears and let it lap milk out of my coffee mug. And when I head back north, I'll peek in the rearview mirror and catch a glimpse of shaggy hair, glowing red eyes, and thick, horrible horns, waiting for me to shape-shift, beastlike, once again. Into what, I'm not sure.

The Poor Woman's Steve Irwin

I'm a dog erection magnet. The neighborhood Fidos take one look at me and pop more stiffies than a seventh-grade health class during an Intro to Lactation unit. Selfishly, I'd like to think this speaks to my general allure; statistically, I know that male dogs spend most of their time erect, with or without my influence. The dog could have spotted a plump corgi from across the street, the kind with the heart-shaped butt that makes 'em want to cruise toward the sex zone at 90 miles per hour. The dog could be excited because they're about to be carried around in a fabulous handbag, or nervous because someone opened a can of Dr Pepper and the bubbles are too loud. The dog could simply be enjoying himself, like during a game of fetch or a viewing of a Jason Statham film.

Some dogs pop erections for no reason at all, if only to remind themselves that they can. Others stay entirely flaccid post-neutering, which I find aesthetically preferable. But sometimes a dog's red alien penis will protrude for a good hour, and you'll find yourself on the phone with your vet while cautiously poking the shiny little mushroom cap with your finger, hissing, "GO BACK, GO BACK INSIDE YOUR PENIS HOUSE." You'll do this because you're afraid that your dog suffers from paraphimosis, or the inability to retract one's penis back into its sheath, a diagnosis you've made after frantically googling "everlasting dog boner," along with "how long can dog have erection," "record for longest dog erection," and "Guinness world record entry form for dogs."

Your vet will assure you that your dog can retract his penis; he probably just doesn't want to. Your vet will also tell you that it's probably a good idea to consider neutering, which is something you've dreaded since you adopted the dog from your college pot dealer, a massive pervert who moved to Saudi Arabia and left the dog at your apartment with a chain leash, a tiny dog shirt, and a wooden door sign that reads A HOUSE IS NOT A HOME WITHOUT A BOSTON TERRIER. That Boston Terrier was Turtle.

Turtle showed up at my door with a distinct hunch, a pair of eyes facing opposite directions, and two bulbous, swinging testicles. From the beginning, he had more problems than most dogs. First, he absolutely lost his mind when he was left alone for more than five minutes. The day after I adopted him, I stopped by on my lunch break to find that he had gnawed away several inches of my bedroom door, knocked over my trash can, sifted through a week's worth of tampons, shredded a Styrofoam ground beef container, jumped onto the kitchen counter, ate half a loaf of banana bread, and spent the rest of his alone time barking with his little pig face smashed up against the window, waiting for me to get home.

Turtle also had a pee problem. Left alone, he urinated on every vertical surface in my one-bedroom apartment, including both of my couch legs and most of the walls. I was unprepared for this behavior. I was raised with female dogs, and up until this point I thought the "marking your territory" thing was a myth. Fortunately, Turtle mostly stuck to hard surfaces and never managed to douse me in his pee, though he did douse my mom once. The incident happened after I hauled him to a nearby park to meet my family. My parents met us near the picnic tables, my dad silent as he feasted on a mass of Big League Chew bubble gum, my mom wearing some sort of caftan per usual. She pointed at the dog and declared, "He is not cute."

She wasn't wrong. Turtle's ribs poked through his dull coat, and he panted to reveal a jack-o'-lantern smile full of missing and broken teeth. He smelled like eggs; he didn't have a tail; his bloodshot eyes were unblinking as he pulled desperately on his leash trying to inspect the leathery frog carcass in the parking lot. He was affectionate but strange; he regularly sprang into people's faces to give sneaky kisses that seemed aggressive to the unaccustomed. He looked a little like the cartoon bat from Disney's *Anastasia*, but less intelligent.

We sat on the ground at Turtle's eye level; my mom eventually warmed up to him, giving him little pats as he stood awkwardly in her lap. My mom then let out a low moan, freezing in place while my dad spat out his Big League Chew. "He's PEEING on her," my dad bellowed. "He's PEEING on your MOTHER!"

My mom's caftan was ruined, and Turtle's reputation was shot. At least, until we discovered that he was connected to the family in one crucial and endearing way: Like the rest of us, Turtle struggled with extreme gastric complications.

The first time Turtle shat in my bed, it was because he ate a discarded cigarette he found on the sidewalk. That was a minor shit—an amuse bouche, really. The second time Turtle shat in my bed, it was because I tried to switch his food from gelatinous gas station Alpo to some kind of wholesome kibble endorsed by Rachael Ray. That was a moderate-to-severe shit; still manageable, if a bit crumbly. But the third time Turtle shat in my bed, it was because he stole a six-day-old coconut cream pie out of the trash can. That night, I walked into my bedroom to find a piping-hot, Wonka-esque chocolate river covering my white duvet and dripping onto my imitation wood floors. I half-expected to find a portly German boy floating helplessly through the stream; alas, all I found was a nervous terrier who was physically incapable of looking me in the eye.

Lucky for me, dog diarrhea hardens insanely quickly. It's like Hershey's Chocolate Shell topping, except it's free, and you don't serve it over ice cream. You serve it over your bedroom shag rug, where it forms a scabby crust and stays put for the rest of your life.

Turtle was just my first introduction to the dog diarrhea/Hershey's Chocolate Shell dichotomy. A few years after adopting him, I signed up to foster another Boston terrier: a ten-month-old female named Olive. Olive had a cruel streak, as evidenced by her Petfinder profile, which carried the following warning labels:

- EXTREMELY PROTECTIVE OF FOOD AND TOYS
- NOT GOOD WITH DOGS
- NOT GOOD WITH CATS
- NOT GOOD WITH KIDS
- HIGHLY INTELLIGENT
- VERY, VERY FAST

Yes, I thought. *This is an ideal pet to bring into my home.*

Surprising absolutely no one, I decided to disregard my own comfort and general sanity in favor of someone else's livelihood— this time, a troubled rescue dog with a bad attitude. I don't know if I did this to be noble, or because I'm not good at sitting quietly with my thoughts. Either way, when I brought Olive to my Chicago apartment to meet Turtle, I wasn't particularly worried. Turtle was a twenty-five-pound bruiser and twice as tall as Olive. Unfortunately, Olive had been tormented by her former owner for months before they dumped her at the pound. While some rescue dogs soften into grateful puddles, others harden themselves to the world, focusing on jailhouse pull-ups and hiding homemade shivs between their tiny dog toenails. Olive was the latter type, and she tried to rip Turtle's throat out almost immediately upon arriving at my apartment.

She then latched on to my ulnar artery and dangled there like a fishing lure while I tried to separate the dogs.

That night, Olive narrowed her eyes, hate filling her heart, and spewed her very own brand of Hershey's Chocolate Shell onto my dining room rug. As I hauled the rug down three flights of stairs to my dumpster, a puddle of terrier diarrhea slid off the rug and onto my downstairs neighbor's porch. By the time I threw my rug in the dumpster, sprinted upstairs for the magic poop spray in my cleaning cabinet, and returned to the neighbor's porch, the diarrhea had already scabbed over, forming a rock-hard crust on the untreated wood grain. It had also dripped between the porch's wooden planks, creating stalactites that were just barely out of reach. I did my best to pick off the foul-smelling droplets, leaving the stalactites to cure in the elements.

Turtle and I withstood two more months of Olive's tyranny, both of us falling prey to her increasingly violent rages. After spending hundreds of dollars for a trainer to tell me that this crap dog needed to be rehomed, I placed Olive with a family on Chicago's west side. The family consisted of two Polish-speaking parents and one adult son, who served as their translator. The son explained that his parents had always wanted a Boston terrier, which his father saw as the "ultimate American dog." I explained that this one was a real dud, which made her even more quintessentially American. The Polish patriarch immediately hoisted her up like a prized squash and declared: "Beautiful."

I chucked Olive's food into the family's kitchen, hustled out the door, and sped away before they could change their minds.

I never spoke to Olive's adopters again, but if you hear of a family annihilator terrorizing Chicago's Polish borough, make sure to take a good look at the local terriers. If you see a tiny girl dog clad in a distressed leather jacket, picking her teeth with someone's disembodied Polish tibia, you'll know exactly what happened.

I'm always doing this. I'm always getting stuck with the most problematic members of the animal kingdom. I'd like to blame it on my naturally charitable nature—give me your tired, your poor, your huddled terriers yearning to release an Uno Attack–style stream of feces in the TJ Maxx home decor section—but I think there's just something weak in my nature that attracts these creatures. I am the poor woman's Steve Irwin, tasked with wrangling unruly and dangerous wildlife. Like Steve Irwin, my attention to these animals seems preordained, my fascination with them bordering on my own destruction. I'm a sucker for a pair of dumb dog eyes, which is how I've managed to accumulate the absolute worst pets, piling them into my battered yellow Honda Fit like Noah piloting a slime-colored ark of poorly behaved beasts.

It's not just dogs. The phenomenon extends to all kinds of wildlife. Critters are obsessed with my third-floor walk-up apartment, which is full of both vintage charm and mouse sanctuaries. I've lived there since the summer of 2019, an era when spiking Chicago temperatures left me typing in the nude, butt sweat pouring into my office chair, trying to convince myself my full-body sheen was charming, like Renée Zellweger in *Cold Mountain*. It took me about a week to install one of those large rolling air conditioners—the kind that sits in front of the window and has a hole in the back that allows exhaust to escape. I adhered a flexible three-foot pipe to the back of the machine, allowing the exhaust to flow freely out of the apartment. The thing worked great, and I was finally able to relax in my formerly hellish living room. That is, until realized that the air conditioner was haunted.

Shortly after installing the unit, I heard ghostly scratches coming from the exhaust pipe. The scratches would start faintly, grow louder, and stop after a minute or two. I ignored the scratches for a couple of days, until, sufficiently freaked out, I approached the air conditioner unit with a hammer. I was ready to exorcize the spirit, which I pictured as an old prospector. In my mind, the prospector's ghost resented my air conditioner and really missed the sight of me Porky Pigging around, airing out my clammy buns while clad only in a T-shirt that read HOW ABOUT WE GO BACK TO MY PLACE FOR A CHICAGO-STYLE HOT DOG.

I began the ceremony, humming and running my hands mystically over the pipe. "Be gone, spirit," I whispered, giving the exhaust pipe a gentle tap with my hammer. At that point, a truly enormous squirrel shot out of the exhaust pipe and onto a tree branch outside my window. It had scuttled into the pipe from outside, no doubt seeking respite from the heat of the day. I screamed and leapt back, while the squirrel whipped around menacingly and chattered at me, irate, as if to say, "*Sleep with one eye open, because I'm coming for those clammy buns.*"

Rather than place some kind of barrier between the tree and the exhaust pipe, I now live in fear of the squirrel, hoping it will tire of its tube house and go on to haunt someone else's exhaust pipe. The squirrel returns every summer, scuttling into the pipe to enjoy some free air-conditioning. Sometimes I'll peer out my window to the pipe's opening and see a bushy tail blowing in the exhaust. I do absolutely nothing to remedy the situation. I exist to please the squirrel.

For four years, I existed to please Turtle. Turtle's unique play style could only be described as that of a four-legged bowling ball covered in razor wire, and it got him unofficially banned from every dog park in the city of Chicago. Shortly after moving to the city, I found myself barefoot and filthy, chasing Turtle across the vast expanse of the dog beach as he tried to kill a wild-eyed Australian shepherd. I've seen Turtle bat a Pekingese named Coco around like a furry mosquito; I've pulled Turtle off a rotund pit bull named Ivan, who cowered in fear at my dog's *Million Dollar Baby*–style provocations. Other than Olive, the only dog that's ever stood up to Turtle was another Boston terrier who tried to stick his tongue directly into the scar where Turtle's testicles used to be. This disturbed Turtle so greatly that it was as if the dog had pressed a testicular "off" switch, sending him slinking home into a shameful slumber.

Please do not get me wrong: Turtle loved to play with other dogs. The issue was that Turtle was an inherently dominant creature, which I imagine had something to do with the fact that he was raised by my old drug dealer in a fraternity house. So, convinced that I had learned from the Olive situation, I decided to get Turtle a friend. That's how I found myself scraping diarrhea off my neighbor's porch a second time, this time because of a chunky beagle with very short legs. This beagle was Olive's polar opposite in nearly every way. His foster mom told me he was a "Robin looking for his Batman"—a submissive, timid little man who needed a more confident dog to show him the ropes. I took Turtle to meet him in an enclosed tennis court, where they sniffed each other for a moment until Turtle snarled, ran a frantic circle around the shivering beagle, then looked up at me, satisfied. I brought the beagle home and named him Archie. He's still here, damn it.

When I decided to adopt a second dog, I had this idyllic picture of animal coexistence, like those memes of tortoises and capybaras blissfully sharing a watermelon. I pictured Turtle and Archie chasing each other around the house, keeping each other company, licking each other's feet, throwing wild dog ragers when I left for work, living to the age of sixteen, dying within moments of each other, and leaving me with some peace and quiet for the first time in my life. My friends with live-in partners sold me this fantasy. They told me that having two dogs is just like having one dog—easier, in fact, because they keep each other entertained. Listen to me: When you live alone, having two dogs is not like having one dog. Having two dogs is just endless shitting, all day, forever. Having two dogs goes like this, schedule-wise:

7:30 a.m.: Archie hops down from the bed and watches me expectantly. The second he sees my eyes open, he releases a series of howls to let me know he needs to potty. I try to coax Turtle off of the bed so he, too, can potty, but he's not having it. Turtle stays in bed. Archie has to poop—I know this because he's a little hunched over—but will not poop. He pees, then runs back upstairs, screaming the entire way in an attempt to rouse the neighbors and inform them that he is, in fact, a beagle.

7:33 a.m.: I meet Archie upstairs and find Turtle shivering by the back door, waiting to potty. I throw Archie inside the apartment, run downstairs with Turtle, and let him pee. Archie screams the entire time.

7:35 a.m.: Turtle and I meet Archie upstairs, where he is bellowing for breakfast at an astonishing decibel. I feed Archie two-thirds of a cup of his special diet kibble, because he has gained eight pounds in my possession. I put Turtle's kibble on the ground, but he is not hungry yet and Archie tries to steal it. I chase Archie away and put Turtle's food on the counter.

7:41 a.m.: I make my coffee, and the dogs go to relax in the sunbeam in my office. I pop into the bathroom and clean myself up. I leave the bathroom to find that Archie has left a massive, curly dump on the bottom shelf of my bookcase. I don't know how he managed this, but I imagine that it involved propping himself up on his front legs in a wheelbarrow formation. Turtle rolls his eyes at me. Archie screams.

12:15 p.m.: I take both dogs out for their lunchtime walk. We have to go north, because if we go south we'll pass Pauline's Diner. We can't get anywhere near Pauline's because the manager slipped the dogs bacon a few times last month, and Archie cannot handle the temptation of nearby bacon. If we get within a half mile of Pauline's, Archie will shimmy out of his no-escape Ruffwear harness, sprint away in the nude, and sit in front of Pauline's screaming until Turtle and I catch up with him and I physically hoist both dogs away. So we go north. Archie bounces from one side of the sidewalk to the other like a chunky pinball; Turtle snarls at every dog we pass; Archie finds a dead rat in the alley and rolls on it; Turtle tries to carry the dead rat away clenched between his remaining teeth; I rip the dead rat out of Turtle's mouth and get a little bit of rat juice on me; Archie poops; I pick up the poop; Turtle poops; Archie steps directly in Turtle's poop before I can pick it up; I drag both dogs home, one of them covered in rat guts and the other with an entire turd stuck to his foot. Archie screams.

1:10 p.m.: Dogs go back to sleep in the sunbeam. I am allowed to work for several hours.

4:50 p.m.: Archie wakes and screams for dinner. I deliver both dogs' kibble and frantically slip into my running shoes while they eat. I squeeze them both into their harnesses, which look like little bras. I take them on their second walk of the day. I do my best to avoid the downstairs neighbor who smells like clay and calls them "doggos." My dogs aren't doggos. They are cowboys.

5:45 p.m.: The dogs and I get home, and it is time for our nightly conversation. At this time, I ask the dogs a series of questions while they stare at me, unblinking. My queries include:

- "What business do you have here?"
- "Are you a little man?"
- "Are you a little naked man?"
- "I am hoping to get in touch with a little naked man. Do you know any?"
- "Was today's kibble to your liking?"
- "Last night, did you fart so frequently that the entire bedroom now smells like a discount colonic practitioner's office?"

6:01 p.m.: The dogs want to sit on the porch. I open the door so they can sit on the porch.

6:04 p.m.: The dogs want to come inside. I open the door so they can come inside. I watch TV and browse the internet for items to buy the dogs, like little socks and stuffed hedgehogs.

9:15 p.m.: I get into the shower, leaving the door open so the dogs can protect me from ghosts. Archie accidentally pushes his squishy bone under the couch. He screams for five minutes straight until I creep out of the shower, naked and sopping wet, to retrieve the squishy bone for him.

10:30 p.m.: By the time I'm ready for bed, both of the dogs have claimed spots near my pillows. I slide in between them, their collective fifty pounds squeezing me from both sides like the trash compactor in *A New Hope*. I fall asleep to the sound of their thunderous snores and accept the fact that this is my reality for approximately the next decade of my life.

This was our routine until Turtle died, the result of a very brief and very expensive battle with dog cancer. Before Turtle got sick, I constantly lamented how badly I wanted these things out of my house. I was exhausted. I googled "beagle life expectancy" twice a week. And yet they delighted me. The dogs made me laugh, which helped me laugh at myself. They made me get up and take a walk when I had been stewing in self-loathing for five hours. They were a testament to the fact that it's okay to lie around all day and not *make* anything. When you're a dog, you're a cherished member of the family whether or not you can interpret a Google Sheet. That healed me a little.

When I first brought Turtle home, I was pretty confident that he would fall right into my list-making, scheduled life. I was ready to hack the dog ownership thing. But dogs don't do rituals. Dogs don't do obsessive thoughts. Dogs do garbage. Dogs are genuinely disgusting and will drive you insane. They are imbeciles who'll do anything for a sweet potato. They're the antithesis of perfection. And little by little, I was becoming okay with that—until Turtle got sick, and I realized that most things are out of my control. Before Turtle got sick, I thought I knew exactly what I needed to do to keep him and Archie alive. I wasn't fretting over whether they liked me or enjoyed my company; I was chasing them around trying to keep them from accidentally flinging themselves out of a window. They ruined my life daily, but I liked it that way.

After Turtle got sick, I spent a long time in the Bargaining stage of grief ("I'll never glare at a stranger in the Wendy's drive-thru again if my dog recovers!"). I looked for actions I could take, rituals I could implement, old superstitions I could resurface to somehow save his little body. And still I found myself inconsolable while the vet filled Turtle's vein catheter with the fluid that would stop his heart. Archie waited at home (screaming, probably) while this woman I had never met explained to me that, no, Turtle wouldn't feel a thing, and, yes, he might pee himself a little. That was Turtle's penultimate joke, I think. His final joke was the fact that he didn't close his eyes while he was slipping away, leaving me to cradle the world's most insane-looking dog corpse. Actually, no—his final, *final* joke was leaving me alone with Archie, the screaming beagle that I suspect Turtle always hated a little bit.

Now, it's me and Archie. He screams less frequently, which is I think is because he prefers life as an only child. All this time, he'd been waiting for Turtle to croak so he could get me to himself. He also screams less frequently because I'm getting better at saying no. He's still spoiled rotten—he had a difficult past, and he deserves it—but I've figured out that we're both happier if I put my foot down now and again. *No* to midday trips to Pauline's to get bacon; *no* to standing in the middle of the dark kitchen screaming for dessert at 1 a.m. when I've gone to bed. I've trained him; he's trained me.

Neither of us is perfect. Not long ago, he humiliated me at an office picnic. I brought him around, excited to introduce my coworkers to my problematic son. Unfortunately, someone brought popcorn to the picnic. Since I brought him home from the rescue, Archie has been preternaturally obsessed with popcorn. I hardly ever make it because I don't want to deal with him staring me down in an attempt to score a kernel. I assumed he'd be relatively well-behaved at the picnic, but all bets were off the minute my coworker snapped open that bag of Skinny Pop. Archie immediately popped a boner, locking eyes with the bearer of the Skinny Pop. "Lillian," my coworker called. "Your dog is erect."

Again, it wasn't even good popcorn; it was Skinny Pop. But Archie was so excited about the prospect of a kernel that he couldn't help but get a little sexual. Who brings popcorn to a picnic, anyway?

Like Archie, I'm still not as well trained as I should be. My dog screams and pops boners, and I still struggle to say no as frequently as I should. I'm working on it. I've had to employ a training protocol for myself not unlike Archie's obedience classes, enjoying an extra episode of *Vikings* every time I stand up for myself. That said, I'll never be able to say no to a wretched animal in need. I will always be the person with the ragtag band of pets. How could I not be? My parents have four weird dogs in all shapes and sizes. My dad lines them up to eat Chex cereal with him every morning from his armchair. He calls it Chex Time.

Last fall, I took Archie on a long walk through the neighborhood. He did his business with stunning efficiency; he avoided the chewed-up beef jerky on the sidewalk. He extracted nary a turd from the Turd Bush, a neighborhood attraction for lazy dog owners and their defecating canines. Archie was the picture of perfection, a well-trained, loyal beacon of all that Man's Best Friend can be. I glanced down at him; he glanced up, wagging his tail, sitting in a glorious imitation of a kennel club champion. "Somebody deserves some bacon," I declared, steering him toward Pauline's.

Fifty feet from the diner, he slipped out of his harness and sprinted down the sidewalk, flattening his ears against his head in a display of shocking athleticism. He ran through a murky white substance on the sidewalk; he tripped a toddler. I chased him, screaming. He screamed right back.

We're working on it.

Essential Items to Have on Hand When the World Ends

- Three spare asthma inhalers
- Sharpie, for apocalyptic doodles
- Diverse array of stale granola bars
- Book of moderately challenging crossword puzzles, in case the apocalypse is boring
- LifeStraw, in case I need to drink from a puddle without getting dysentery
- Anti-diarrheal pills, in case I get dysentery anyway
- Snakebite survival pamphlet I picked up at the zoo, in case I am set upon by vipers
- Crumpled photo of Bill Nye, for when the aliens ask to meet our king
- Crumbled photo of young Michael Caine, for jacking it
- Extra phone charger, in case I need to make some calls (?)
- Hideous money belt I bought to study abroad in 2015, in case I need to strap my valuables to my lower abdomen while trekking from Safe Zone to Safe Zone
- Cigarettes, for smoking or jamming into mouth for

- lighthearted walrus impression
- Twenty dollars in cash, in case someone, somewhere, still values legal tender after 90 percent of the world's population has perished in a fiery Armageddon
- The physical and mental tenacity to go on where others will not. The innate drive to traverse hostile landscapes and battle roving bands of opportunistic bandits who seek to further deplete an already broken world. The bravery to start anew. To find purpose. To gaze at a barren wasteland and seek what beauty remains.
- Absolute shit ton of tampons

Bugging Out

When the world ends, I'll have the candy. Specifically, a Ring Pop party pack, featuring six lickable jewels in flavors like Watermelon, Sour Cherry, and Very Berry Punch. The party pack is crammed into my bug-out bag, a sturdy canvas backpack I got secondhand from my stylish neighbor. He gave it to me assuming I'd use it as a cute commuting accessory; instead, I've stashed it in the northeast corner of my bedroom, wedged between my radiator and my dresser in a spot that is both discreet and accessible in case of nuclear cataclysm.

I figure we've got about five good years left before the apocalypse. One cursory scroll through social media and it's clear we're doomed, though the exact nature of imminent societal collapse depends on who you ask. Ask an astronomer, and they'll tell you about the phenomenon of orbital instability: the idea that earth is a high-powered dune buggy careening off course, soon to collide with one of its terrestrial neighbors in a horrible blast of atmospheric gases and guts. Ask a climate scientist, and they'll hang their long-suffering head in their long-suffering hands and warn that deforestation will get us unless a supervolcano gets us first. Ask an epidemiologist, and they'll crow about synthetic viruses and publicly accessible genome databases. Ask an Evangelical, and they'll reference the rapture. (Quick Q: Where are we on Christ's method of return? Are we picturing him descending to earth in a slow freefall, like a man-shaped snowflake? Or will His Heavenly Father strap him into a decommissioned U.S. Air Force RQ-4 Global Hawk military aircraft and tell him to brace for impact?)

I've got my own theories. My money's on planetary debris tearing through the stratosphere, breaching the ozone and knocking out the grid with a terrific *kerplunk*. One minute, we earthlings will be going about our business, dozing in marketing meetings and listening to podcasts and making fruit salad; the next, humankind will be tossed asunder by the impact of an asteroid the size of God's fist. The resulting seismic waves will annihilate a third of the earth's population, leaving the rest of us with no means to call our moms or watch reality television.

If it's not an asteroid, it'll be nuclear conflict. And if it's not nuclear conflict, it'll be bugs. Either way, chaos will ensue. World leaders will fall silent, retreating to their apocalypse yachts. Armed marauders will take to the streets, ready to commit heinous acts for a gallon of fuel and a pack of Camels. Our already tenuous society will crumble, leaving any survivors to submit to the primeval currency of blood and gristle. And when that happens, I'll be ready with my bug-out bag.

Building a standard bug-out bag is easy. If you're not sure where to start, the Federal Emergency Management Agency's website has a decent list for amateur preppers. Water, food, batteries, first aid kit. The basics. But to build a truly exceptional bug-out bag, you need a busted brain that is prone to catastrophizing. Reader, I have that—but it wasn't until 2020, when my internal catastrophizing truly peaked, that I was able to channel my panicked cerebrum into a tangible task: building the perfect emergency knapsack.

I lived alone during the height of the pandemic. I was panicked about the state of the world, sick of baking and organizing my sock drawer, and prone to occasional shoplifting (nothing felonious—a Neosporin here, a box cutter there). I had lost the bulk of my income, and everything felt out of control. It was the perfect storm for building the perfect bug-out bag.

The bag came together slowly—a pocket flashlight here, two cans of beans there. Today I've got hand warmers, military-grade protein bars, instant coffee, and one small compass I honestly do not know how to use. I've got a pocket flashlight with extra batteries, three box cutters I accidentally stole from a former employer, and several pairs of the ugliest, most gigantic Hanes underpants you have ever seen. And, of course, the Ring Pops.[*]

Assembling the bag felt good. It was the first time that my penchant for catastrophizing felt empowering, not debilitating. My pandemic anxiety retreated as I assessed my emergency inventory—making a list, checking it twice, then checking it again and again until I felt prepared for every possible hellish outcome. Every time I added a collapsible pup tent or multitool to my sturdy canvas knapsack, I breathed a sigh of relief, convinced I'd staved off another form of apocalyptic demise. (The pup tent would save me from freezing; the multitool would allow me to extract splinters or assist during a breech birth by making a small taint incision.)

This was my first foray into prepping, though I've always been into the apocalypse. My doomsday obsession is an inevitable side effect of growing up in the Ozarks, where serious preppers shell out the big bucks for underground bunkers equipped with shelf-stable

---

* Why Ring Pops? Perhaps I'll need quick fuel to outrun the mutant human-mosquito hybrid creatures that have inherited the earth. Perhaps I'll need to barter with a crazed highwayman who's craving a hit of Red Dye 40. Perhaps I'll live out my entrepreneurial fantasies by opening a postapocalyptic roadside nostalgia museum. I'll face the deserted highway with a bullhorn, standing in front of my ramshackle collection of one-eyed Furbies and stale candy necklaces. "Only nineties kids will remember these!" I'll crow, displaying a handful of glittering Ring Pops to the band of raccoons I've assembled as my chosen family. They'll blink, hiss, and scuttle back into a nearby dumpster.

biscuit mix and military-grade rifles. It's also a natural consequence of my early Evangelical indoctrination, which taught me that Christ will return to claim his chosen people very, very soon. My parents have a refrigerator message that really drives that message home: JESUS IS COMING, it reads. LOOK BUSY.

Impending Rapture aside, I'm eerily skilled at dreaming up worst-case scenarios. I don't remember much from freshman year geometry class, save for the mean girl with scoliosis who spun around in her seat to ask me if my family was *poor*, but I do remember how to write a geometric proof. To write a proof, you have to use something called a conditional statement. Conditional statements have two parts: an "if" statement, and a "then" statement. (Example: *If* I encounter a band of marauders while walking the endless road to a safe zone in the apocalypse, *then* I can ply them with Ring Pops to let me pass.)

My life is a constant flood of conditional statements. On a good day, I can drown out the negotiations, quieting my brain with trash television. But on a bad day, I'm overwhelmed with endless conditional statements that prevent me from making any sort of practical decision. For example:

- **If** I walk through a cloud of pollen on my way to the grocery store, **then** I will need to use my emergency asthma rescue inhaler.

- **If** my emergency asthma rescue inhaler has somehow been punctured in my backpack, **then** I will need to pack a second emergency asthma rescue inhaler.

- **If** I pack a second emergency asthma rescue inhaler but a mugger steals my backpack, **then** I will have wiped out my emergency asthma rescue inhaler stash, forcing me to dip into my *apocalyptic* asthma rescue inhaler stash, which is supposed to be *for the apocalypse.*

Consider that approach, and it's easy to see why I keep a bug-out bag handy. When you're preparing for apocalyptic scenarios, catastrophizing is *good.* Unfortunately, in my mind, anything can be an apocalyptic scenario.

To me, every day is one long string of emergencies. I've angered a fellow motorist: emergency. I've left a small but distinct butt-sweat stain on my chair at work: emergency. I've forgotten my on-the-go beef jerky stash and let my blood sugar dip slightly: emergency. I've recommended a restaurant, and a friend didn't like it: worst emergency imaginable, cataclysmic self-loathing has ensued, must go die now.

In the apocalypse, one wrong move will send you straight into a zombie horde. I am not living through the apocalypse at this time, nor am I currently faced with the prospect of a zombie horde. But for my overactive, overthinking, overprotective brain, making one wrong move—leaving home without my jerky or letting my tires get too low—feels like the end of the world. If I forget to pack my emergency jerky, I'll be directly responsible for the death of a hypoglycemic stranger I meet on the train. If I can't read a map, I can't drive my friends to safety in the event of a nuclear attack. If I step on a crack, I'm single-handedly responsible for breaking my mother's back, and also *your* mother's back, and also probably Barack Obama's mother's back. When you approach a standard-issue social interaction with an apocalyptic mindset, a single miscalculation spells disaster.

Sure, there are perks to compulsively preparing for the very worst. It makes me a good babysitter, a good partner, and a good employee. I never run out of pantry staples. I always have a Band-Aid. I am positively rich in emergency asthma inhalers. Planning for the end of the world is all about anticipating needs—your own, along with everyone else's. It's the perfect gig for someone like me, born curmudgeonly and methodical, reluctantly maternal and perpetually neurotic. The worst iteration of a Virgo, for people who believe in that sort of thing.

There are obvious downsides to catastrophizing. Sharks can smell blood from a quarter of a mile away; freeloaders can smell my hyper-preparedness from even further. By "freeloaders," I mean people—friends, coworkers, love interests—who want someone to anticipate their needs without asking anything in return. I'm a freeloader magnet. They take one look at my oiled-up hatchback and organized pantry and know that I can take care of them. I reward their greedy impulses, picking up strays with the understanding that I alone must carry the weight of the world, even as it hurtles into the sun.

It's a trust thing. My brain balks at risk, and there's nothing riskier than placing your trust in someone else when the apocalypse is at hand. It feels safer to assume the burden of total preparedness. If I keep my bug-out bag stocked, I'll never have to rely on someone else's inferior supplies. If I shoulder the weight of the world, assuming responsibility for every possible outcome, no one can let me down.

Not long ago, I realized my bug-out bag was complete. I conducted a routine inventory check, reorganizing my hand warmers and emergency Sharpies, taking stock of my small collection of emergency ointments, when it hit me: I've got a pretty impressive stash. It's more than enough to sustain me through the apocalypse; possibly even *Apocalypse 2: Radioactive Boogaloo*. I've got portable shelter and heat, enough calories for a few days on the road, and a small arsenal of makeshift weapons that I'm too chicken to actually use. My kit goes way beyond FEMA recommendations, thanks to the aforementioned if-then statements. I had accounted for most basic apocalypse criteria: plague (high-filtration masks), famine (military-grade protein bars, plus a field guide to foraging edible plants), and power grid collapse (compass and map of back roads leading to my parents' place in the Ozark hills). At that point, I did what any savvy prepper might do: I began to dream up even worse possibilities.

I prowled Amazon, pricing out potassium iodide tablets and detailed guides to human anatomy. I googled "how to shoot bow and arrow for girls." I made a short list of unexpected apocalypse triggers, asking myself if I was truly ready for, say, a coordinated grasshopper attack meant to eliminate humankind. An hour later, I emerged from my stupor, checked Instagram, and immediately received an ad for an alt-right doomsday prepping website called My Patriot Supply.

It was time to reenter the world of the living.

The accidental foray into My Patriot Supply forced me to acknowledge that my bug-out bag is, at best, a coping mechanism—and at worst, a way to affirm my own trust issues. I admittedly spent a minute or two scrolling through the site's wares, which range from heirloom seeds to seven-hundred-dollar water filtration systems. The site's tagline said it all: "Trusted Self-Reliance."

In a time of crisis, my bug-out bag helped me feel in control. Realistically, my apocalypse madness won't do any good in the case of the actual apocalypse. I think of the bag as a tiny lifeboat attached to a cruise ship; it won't do any good in a true crisis (if the Carnival deluxe liner is swallowed by a Leviathan with an unnatural hunger for members of the leisure class, for example). The truth is that the world is scary, and I'm just one person who recreationally ventures into the doomsday prepper blogosphere. Coming to terms with the futility of my preparedness has made it easier to accept the truth: that, when the end comes, relying on other people is the only thing that will get me through.

I used to envision the apocalypse in a very specific way. I'd spring into action, piling friends and loved ones into my hatchback and driving them to safety while buildings toppled around us. I'd then use my limited knowledge of seed husbandry to start a farming commune. I'd study medical textbooks and cure infected splinters and figure out how to power a streetlight using only artichoke juice. I'm a more physically capable specimen in these fantasies. I'm 155 pounds of pure muscle, forged in the flames of my makeshift blacksmith operation. (I've also taught myself the art of smelting.) I instinctively know how to swing an ax, gut a fish, and amputate a limb. I've somehow learned the art of tactical driving. I am always wearing eyeliner and very nice cargo shorts.

But the truth is that, even with my penchant for preparedness, I'm just as helpless as the next neurotic apartment dweller. I can stockpile all the waterproof fire starters and confusing compasses in the world, but if a hostile alien race comes to claim Lake Michigan, I'll panic right along with everyone else. Same goes for the more likely scenario in which climate change slowly boils our insides until we're nothing but burbling puddles on the ground. If/when that occurs, my stash of emergency batteries is worth absolutely nada.

In a way, that's freeing. Just because I *can* plan for the worst doesn't mean I have to. Fixating on some dark future won't keep the sky from falling. I'd rather channel that energy into an interesting hobby, like forming a heist crew, or treasure hunting, or licking a Ring Pop until my tongue turns an appealing shade of blue that allows me to pop out at my boyfriend and scream, "LIZARD GIRL!"

I'm starting to realize that there's no point in preparing for a future if I have to go it alone. It still takes everything I've got to lean on other people—but it's better than the alternative, which I imagine involves living out my days in a boarded-up cabin with a gas mask strapped over my wild, graying hair. I already know I'm not equipped to walk the lonely doomsday road by myself, Cormac McCarthy–style. When you find a community that makes riding out the apocalypse seem a bit more bearable, you've got to cling to that.

In releasing my dogged self-reliance, I've managed to cultivate a

community. It's not so far-fetched to think that, in a worst-case scenario, they'd anticipate my needs, and I'd anticipate theirs. Maybe
we'd take turns carrying the bug-out bags, allowing the others to
rest. I mean, *really* rest.

Either way, I can now stride boldly into the apocalypse—which,
let's face it, is likely hours away—knowing that someone out there
will very likely share their emergency candy stash with me. Even if
I have nothing to give in return.

I Am Backpack Pug

I once met a pug who wears a little backpack. He trundled down my street one afternoon, tugging at his cheetah-print leash with a determined glint in his eye, furry rolls sloshing from side to side like a half-full can of cranberry sauce. He glanced at me as if to say, "Hello, lady." I knelt down to give him a pat and inspected the backpack, which was fastened snugly under his belly. "What does he have in there?" I asked his owner. She glanced up from her phone and shrugged. "Nothing," she replied. "He just likes to have a little job. Makes him feel useful, I think."

I, too, like to have a little job. Ideally, a few little jobs. Historically, I feel better about myself when I'm securing restaurant reservations, planning a birthday party, researching ethical wasp removal practices, or coaching a friend through a breakup. Preferably, all four at once. Why? Because I need to feel useful in order to feel valuable. It's an enduring insecurity, one that's plagued me since I learned I could clap erasers for extra credit. I am backpack pug.

I've always assumed people-pleasing was my destiny. I'm the bossy, fretting big sister of two much younger siblings. Once I was tall enough to reach the microwave, I was put to work as their baby-sitter, positioned as a role model and disciplined via ruthless Texan spankings if I complained about it. Most of the time, I'd plop my brother and sister in front of the TV so I could go write venomous screeds in my unicorn journal or covertly reread the sex scene from *Atonement.* "Do *not* tell Mom and Dad," I warned, sticking my finger in my siblings' round Moon Pie faces. "Or I will make a *hibachi dinner* of your *ass.*"

My parents were no stricter than my friends' folks. My spank-ings were of the open-handed variety, never with belt or switch. For the most part, I was allowed to dress how I liked. Even my academic indoctrination was relatively mild, although it did begin early. My dad used to run me through my times tables in the mornings en route to elementary school, but he'd always reward me with brief interludes from the Foreigner CD in his glovebox. "It's 'Double Vi-sion' time for geniuses," he'd declare, proudly snapping his fingers.

Nevertheless, by the time I reached high school, I had become an insufferable goody-two-shoes. My friends snuck out to parties and tried cool drugs; I stayed home, rereading my grandma's tat-tered Janet Evanovich novels, eating low-fat peach frozen yogurt, and dreaming up ways to win over those around me. I won my par-ents' appreciation via good grades; I won my teachers' respect via an overloaded extracurricular schedule that emphasized my natu-ral leadership skills and lifelong fear of marijuana. I won my peers' acceptance by shedding my skin between classes and hangouts, slipping stealthily into whatever type of personality was most likely to garner external approval in any given scenario. To the Key Club, I was a humanitarian with boundless energy for aggressive Salva-tion Army bell-ringing. To the Drama Club, I was a clown, cracking jokes in an attempt to secure a choice role in *Seussical: The Musical.* To the Pep Squad, I was a die-hard sports fan capable of hiding the fact that I did not, and probably never will, understand the rules of American football. "DOES THAT MEAN WE WIN," screamed my best friend after the first tackle of the game. "YES ALMOST CERTAINLY," I screamed back, lifting my shirt to reveal the school mascot painted across my abdomen. The only social group I couldn't penetrate was the Party Crowd. Once again: scared of pot.

For all my social anxiety, you'd think I was brought up by ogres who beat me with tree limbs. You'd think that I was bullied relentlessly, harangued by beautiful preteens until I learned to disguise my awkward impulses, or that I was indoctrinated by a flagellant church, taught to mar my own flesh at the merest whisper of sin. But I wasn't. Yes, I was raised Evangelical; yes, my parents employed semiregular corporal punishment; yes, a middle school classmate once used my pubescent flab as an excuse to digitally disinvite me from her annual pool party. ("Fat people shouldn't wear swimsuits," she typed over AOL Instant Messenger. Her signature read ~*~GURL P0W3R~*~.)

But I still have no idea exactly when or why the people-pleasing took root. Save any unmistakable external influence, I'm forced to conclude that I did it to myself. There's a strong chance that I, wrapped up in my own insecurity, planted the people-pleasing seed—a strong chance that I watered it, placed it in direct sunlight, and watched it grow into a giant, spindly ficus that tangled me in its roots and trapped me in my self-imposed role as Girl of the Year. In my mind, people-pleasing was the only way to feel safe, to quiet my fears that I was born unworthy. It was only by completing a never-ending conveyer belt of duties that I'd somehow earn my place in the world. Now here I am, three decades into a life full of unpaid catsitting, therapeutic listening, and midnight baking for people I don't even like that much.

It's not all bad. I genuinely enjoy making restaurant reservations, a task that allows me to skew the evening in favor of mozzarella sticks. I'm also an uncannily skilled planner, capable of booking family vacations with the single-minded assurance of an overzealous IRS agent. I accept these duties happily most of the time, partly because a well-planned evening is an act of love and partly because, like a pug wearing a backpack, I'm excited to have a little job. Unfortunately, when you're in charge of everything, it feels perilously easy to let people down. Consider the time that I steered myself, my mom, and my sister into a dining experience straight out of the Book of Revelation. We had made the sacred pilgrimage to Florida in search of beachfront loungers on which to roast our skin to the approximate crispness of a Peking duck. There, we spent our days in peak womanly form: lying silent and grimacing on our loungers, bikini tops untied, flipping from back to belly and back again every twenty minutes to ensure an even broil. We spent our nights at restaurants that I painstakingly researched, most of which worked out fine. Unfortunately, dazed by light sun poisoning, I made one ill-advised reservation at Silas Dent's Steakhouse & Bayside Bar. There we sat, three lobster-colored blond women with saltwater-crispy hair, in a restaurant that looked like the set of *Twin Peaks* if *Twin Peaks* had been shot inside a flooded coal mine. The light was greenish and sickly; the walls were covered with maritime artifacts including an uninhabited scuba suit that hung morbidly from a hook on the ceiling. I realized that the Yelpers who had left the positive reviews—"Great for groups!" read one; "Fun nautical decor!!!" read another—were almost certainly vision-impaired geriatrics enjoying their last meal en route to the glue factory.

I gingerly poked the Billy Mouth Bass on the wall next to our booth, which made a droning sound that sounded a lot like "hyyyy-eeeeeeelp." I peered at the bass. "Silas, is that you?" I whispered, concerned that the Billy Mouth Bass was inhabited by Silas Dent's lost soul. "Silas, are you trapped in there." The fish's wailing ceased, and we were left with the eerie squeaking from a plastic stingray that swung above our table like a chandelier. We perused the menu, which was available only via View-Master. I clicked through the entrées and landed on an ahi tuna steak, which arrived grayish and foreboding, somehow rock-hard and rubbery at the same time. My sister ate a few hush puppies and spent the rest of the time passive-aggressively turning a sea captain's wheel that hung on the wall next to the booth. After the meal, our server delivered the check along with a red plastic tray. "Your palate cleansers," she grinned, presenting the tray with a flourish. On the tray were three tiny ice cream cones, each filled with orange sherbet.

I agonized over this experience for weeks, worried that I had robbed us of a pleasant evening. Never mind that my mother and sister are both adults perfectly capable of making restaurant reservations; it was my job, it had always been my job, and I had beefed it. I was in charge of everything, which meant taking responsibility for things that weren't my fault.

As evidenced by the rubbery tuna, people-pleasing also gets you into some disgusting situations. Consider the time that I, ever the dutiful daughter, shaved my mother's matronly beaver. This was years before the Dent's incident; I was still in high school, and I had just won a superlative award for Most Spirited Senior, so I was riding pretty high. My dad had already squired my siblings to the beach, leaving my mom and me alone in the room to change into our swimsuits. I slipped into my tankini and waited for my mom to get changed, staring out of the window at a gaggle of good-looking European men in the tropical courtyard below. That's when I heard my mom bellow from the bathroom. "Lillian, get in here!" she shouted, as I reluctantly tore myself away from ogling the beachgoing foreigners.

Upon entering the bathroom, I was faced with every daughter's nightmare: my mom, holding a disposable razor *American Gothic*–style, clad in a one-piece bathing suit with an impossibly lush mass of pubic hair flowing out of her suit.

"I'd do it myself, but my back hurts from the flight," she said calmly. I stared at her in disbelief. She then gestured grandly to her crotch and gave me my marching orders: "Shave me."

I balked, though only for a moment. The possibility of grooming the pubic mound from which you, yourself, emerged is enough to fill even the most obedient daughter with visceral disgust. My hesitation passed when my mom tapped her foot impatiently and handed me a bar of soap. Speechless, I grabbed the razor, lathered the soap onto a washcloth, and began to shave my mother's pubes.

Minutes later, I was covered in 'em. I blinked and saw pubes floating gently all around me, an oddly serene crotchal snowfall. I had pubes on my shirt. I had pubes in my eye. I was choking on pube dust, sputtering like someone who'd just walked through a powdered sugar factory without a protective mask. The result was a crude, patchy hack job. It was very *The Gift of the Magi*—like my mom had sliced off her pubes and sold them to some brutal wig maker on an ill-fated Christmas Eve. She checked my work with a hand mirror and nodded, satisfied.

I didn't even make it to the beach that day. I was too grossed out to do anything other than stand beneath the showerhead and stare blankly at the wall. It's just like Christ said: When you saw only one set of footprints in the sand, it's because I was in the shower, hosing off my mom's pubes.

At some point, my people-pleasing tendencies became an irritating form of martyrdom. As I advanced into my twenties, I found myself behaving like Giles Corey, the farmer executed during the Salem Witch Trials after failing to own up to his status as a Satan-smooching warlock. Corey's wife was strung up along with the other accused witches, but Corey suffered a far more dramatic fate: suffocation by stones. His accusers, ever innovative, adjusted the brims of their little Puritan hats and piled large stones onto Corey's chest until he died. Legend has it that Corey, defiant until the end, jeered at his executioners as they crushed his sternum. "More weight!" he cried as the stones stacked up. "MORE WEIGHT!"

I imagine that Giles Corey felt pretty silly about his last words. The thrill of martyrdom tends to fade when you feel your sternum crack under the weight of a mossy boulder. As my own Giles Coreyfication advanced, I realized that my martyrdom had metastasized far beyond helpful territory. I wasn't people-pleasing for others; I was doing it for myself. People-pleasing isn't goodness—it's the performance of goodness, which demands that others bear witness and congratulate me for being so selfless.

I craved the praise that came after throwing a friend a water bottle from the trunk of my car. "You're a lifesaver," they'd groan, chugging my last Aquafina as I looked on, parched. I needed the affirmation that I garnered taking on extra tasks at work. "Lillian's so dependable," my supervisor would say as I picked up the slack for yet another coworker, completing my nauseating performance of Grown-Up Teacher's Pet. "Such a good daughter," my mom assured me, patting my hand as I picked her pubes out of my eyelashes. Every time someone praised me for putting my own needs last, I'd lap it up, a smile stretched tight across my exhausted face.

Eventually, I cracked. I had planned a trip abroad with a passive-aggressive boyfriend, testing the limits of my spreadsheet prowess in an attempt to pack maximum cultural enrichment into a ten-day period. The museums were lovely, the countryside picturesque—but all I could think about was visiting a storybook town that was nestled in the bosom of the Austrian Alps and accessible only by boat. I fantasized about strolling through the cobblestone streets, peering inside candy-colored houses with my handsome boyfriend on one side and some sort of busty Austrian grog wench on the other. "BOYFRIEND VERY HANDSOME," the grog wench would bellow, siphoning grog into my mouth via a discreet tube. It would be the perfect end to a perfect trip, made so by my foolproof planning.

The day we were booked to visit the town, it stormed. "No boats," grunted our gruff Airbnb host, offering us a plate of rock-hard bread. We were left to watch the lightning from our sweltering flat, scowling at each other and eating cheese pizza topped with corn. My travel companion didn't bother to hide his annoyance with me. By this point, it had been established that I was the planner in the relationship. I had booked all our lodgings, all our flights, all our train and bus travel—but I had failed to plan for poor weather and, thus, had single-handedly ruined our trip.

I didn't volunteer to plan the vacation, exactly; I just had enough experience to know that the burden of planning was mine to bear. Spend enough time quietly shouldering every burden, and people will inevitably come to expect it of you. Turns out, if one person handles an entire relationship's worth of administrative work, it'll come to light when you're living out of a suitcase and traveling by train while stoned Berliners blast techno music from the sleeper car.

I could've stood up for myself. I could've told my boyfriend to shove it, that I resented my unspoken role as a trumped-up secretary left to plan our relationship while he sat on his bony hind end, fretted over his art, and blasted Fugazi at an unprecedented volume. I could've engaged in the barest amount of self-reflection and realized that I am in no way uniquely tasked with managing the needs of everyone in my immediate vicinity. That level of self-reflection felt a bit out of reach—but I could feel a chip in my cheery exterior, threatening to crack me wide open like a pebble on a windshield. Like Giles Corey, I was struggling to breathe, struggling to maintain my composure as the keeper of all.

Over time, I formed more cracks. I overbooked my social calendar, sometimes scheduling two morning coffee hangouts before 9 a.m. I lost track of the details of friends' lives, letting them all blur together in one amorphous blob. I was a little like a serial Tinder dater, rushing from social engagement to social engagement and mixing up people's names in the process. I found myself jetting across town in my beat-up Trailblazer, sneaking away from a 4:30 p.m. happy hour in an attempt to make a six o'clock dinner scheduled by an acquaintance with whom I had absolutely nothing in common. Meaningful connections were traded for the quick hits of dopamine that came every time I checked a friend off my to-do list. I'd walk away from coffee dates and wine tastings and happy hours and clap my hands in satisfaction as if I'd just completed an unsavory errand. "That's that handled," I'd say—until the next time someone insisted that we *must* catch up, which generally involved me sitting quietly as they crowed about their condo drama.

In the hubbub, I lost track of myself. I became spineless and tasteless in the pursuit of agreeability, a wet marshmallow of a woman flattened by the weight of the world. I cheered for friends' sports teams and assured coworkers that I'd be honored to watch their ugly babies, free of charge. Chipper agreement became my baseline. "Don't you hate it when Angela does that *thing*?" an acquaintance would ask. I'd blink, look up from my third social coffee of the day, and nod frantically. "Yes abso*lutely* she is the *worst*." *Never mind that I couldn't* remember who Angela was or what kind of thing she did. At the end of the coffee date, the acquaintance would squeeze my hand. "You always know exactly what to say," they'd squeal, skipping away with the confidence of someone who'd just spent an hour being superficially affirmed by someone with the resolve of a sea sponge.

I landed in therapy after dumping the passive-aggressive Fugazi boyfriend, who I assume has now tasked someone else with coordinating his joy. My goal: to rebuild my personality from scratch without accounting for the preferences of people around me. Turns out, that's really hard to do. I started slow, playing a game I called "Good or Bad." I'd walk down the sidewalk, zero in on things within my reach, and attempt to determine if I liked those things without bowing to external influence. I'd pass a woman with bubble gum–pink hair and force myself to assess the hair, asking myself: GOOD or BAD?

In the Giles Corey times, my assessment would rely entirely on someone else's expectations. Would my parents find the hair GOOD or BAD? Would my love interest like it? What about past love interests, or future love interests? What about my landlord? Would he like the Double Bubble hair? Only after considering everyone else's preferences would I consider my own. At that point, it was impossible to determine what was *me, really*, and what was *me, subconsciously watered down* by everyone else taking up space in my brain.

I'm back now. Finally. After many, many rounds of GOOD or BAD, I learned to determine that I like the pink hair. I like the overpriced flowers at the farmers' market. I like the frozen cauliflower rice from Trader Joe's. I like the twee pop music playing in the coffee shop. I can, on occasion, ask someone else to make the restaurant reservations. Imagine.

This world makes it very hard for women to accept our interests and desires and instincts. Everyone seems excited to tell us about all the better, more palatable ways to be. In a world like that, people-pleasing is often easier than striding boldly forth to account for one's own preferences. To be everybody's favorite is to ignore your gut, to dismiss the things you feel so strongly in your bones. If you don't feel strongly about anything, you can slip into being everybody's favorite with ease. And if you're everybody's favorite—if you work yourself to collapse to prove yourself indispensable, capable of heading off the world's disasters, inequities, and minor discomforts—no one can throw you away. Right?

Right?

More weight.

When your value is determined by your usefulness and malleability, it leaves little room to mess up. Booking a reservation at a scary fish restaurant becomes a disaster, another way to fail those around you and confirm your own inadequacy. Fortunately, *dispensable* doesn't have to mean "disposable." I don't assess my peers based on their usefulness in social scenarios. It stands to reason, then, that they'd love me even if I didn't have emergency bottled water locked and loaded at all times. That I am safe, even if I express an idea or a preference or a need.

Today, I feel safe. My sister and I still laugh about Silas Dent's, reminiscing on the singular thrill of navigating an entire dinner menu via View-Master. When we're apart and missing each other, I'll shoot her a sinister text with two words, no context, and no punctuation: Silas Dent's. She'll text back: omg stop.

Last August, my boyfriend and I squabbled good-naturedly over which movie to watch. He chose *Broadcast News*; I chose *Jennifer's Body*. Initially, I conceded, terrified to make the case for what I believe to be Megan Fox's single greatest cinematic achievement. "Do you really want to watch *Broadcast News*?" he asked, shredding my superficial protestations. He looked at me, eyebrows raised, as if to say: *I know you. I know you, and I see what you're doing.* God, it makes my stomach hurt.

I met his gaze for a second before I glanced away, sheepish. "Well," I stuttered, pointing to the calendar and trying to think of a way to advocate for my pick without outwardly expressing a preference. "It *is* August. And *Jennifer's Body* is really more of a back-to-school movie."

He grinned and pressed play. Enter Megan Fox. I leaned back into the couch, stunned. How strange that my interests—specifically, my interest in watching Megan Fox light her tongue on fire—are just as worthy as anyone else's.

I'm a B$_{12}$ Bitch Now

Angela, *hi*. So good to see you, but I'm sorry it's under such *devastating* circumstances. I just can't believe your mother's gone. *Beautiful* funeral, gorgeous eulogies. Of course, I can't help but wonder—was your mother by any chance taking B$_{12}$? It's a vitamin. Not sure if you've ever heard of it. Maybe it would have helped.

Me? Oh, *God*, I've been taking B$_{12}$ for *ages*. I needed a little pick-me-up after I decided to stop donating to the Watoto Children's Choir—*stunning* children, but where is the vibrato?—and a gal in my Airedale terrier trafficking Facebook group recommended B$_{12}$. That first dose had me feeling more invigorated than the time I sat on my balance ball, sniffed a toasted marshmallow candle, and watched the scene in *Heavyweights* in which the little fat boys slather the Scandinavian fitness coach in honey. Angela, I felt *good*. Hand me a canapé.

Of course, there are several different ways to consume B$_{12}$. You can take it as a pill, you can take it intravenously, you can bathe in it at a subterranean spa in TriBeCa—it's impossible to get in, the receptionist is a cursed Easter Island statue—but I like to take it in liquid form. I carry it in this little glass vial—you like it? It's small, like my *waist*—so I can slurp down a dose during stressful situations. Like last week, when I found out that my housekeeper has been hiding the Russian Imperial Romanov family in her bucket bag this entire time. Or last October, when I gave my severed clitoris to a traveling merchant in exchange for a new high-efficiency clothes dryer and realized a second too late that it wasn't even *front-loading*.

Angela, let me be clear: I'm never *not* taking B_{12}.

Some people caution me against taking too much, but I'll let you in on a little secret: You physically cannot take too much. Your body just releases the B_{12} that it doesn't use. Guess where that goes? Angela, it goes into your *urine*. Then, of course, you can siphon the *urine* back into your mouth, thus ingesting even more B_{12}. Not sure how to sterilize *urine*? Listen, have you tried using B_{12}? Just an idea.

B_{12} makes you strong. B_{12} boosts your mood. B_{12} will convince your gut bacteria to form a *blissful* family band. Oh, you already have too much gut bacteria? I . . . have an idea for you? It's . . . called B_{12}? Just a thought, Angela.

Take a good look at your mother's embalmed corpse, Angela. Now, look at me. She's surrounded by pungent sprays of funereal blooms, and I'm oozing the *vigor* of a twenty-one-year-old Baptist camp counselor.

Oh, you couldn't afford camp as a child? Did . . . you try B_{12}?

Your left nostril is whistling because there's a tiny man in there and he is *not* paying his property taxes? B_{12}. Wage gap prevented you from purchasing one of those giant foam cowboy hats, leaving you with nothing to wear to the Homeowners Association Hoedown? B_{12}. Elizabeth Warren didn't get enough talking time during the first Democratic debate? Scream, then take some B_{12}.

Oh, *dear*—it looks like your mother's bloated, ashen corpse has fallen out of her coffin, crushing two of the caterers beneath her dead bulk! Look, that one's trying to speak. What is it, dear? What do you require? Call . . . call an ambulance? Don't be silly! Angela, hand me my B_{12}.

Angela, you're growing red in the face. Oh, look at that—your hands are around my *neck*! Oh, Angela, look at your *cuticles*. Have you tried putting a little B_{12} on those? (GAG) Just a thought. I must say, Angela, you really have quite a firm (GAG) grip! My, I'm feeling a bit (GAG) dizzy. Can you (GAG) pass me my GAG GAG GAG GAG GAG GAG GAG GAG

Angela, *hi*! I appear to have ascended from my body after that tricky choking incident. Good news: My constant B_{12} consumption has guaranteed me a place among the heavenly bodies. I *know*. Just one quick thing before I embrace an eternity of celestial splendor—can you pass me my B_{12}?

Just a thought!

Face of an Angel,
Heart of a Gerbil

I turned to my two best friends, thoughtfully chewing one half of a cafeteria Bosco Stick. "Guys, am I hot, cute, or classically beautiful?" I asked, mouth full of cheesy dough. They barely looked up from their lunches; seventh graders only had twenty-five-minute lunch periods, which was hardly enough time to savor a pack of Scooby-Doo Mystery Machine gummies. Anyway, this wasn't an unusual question; we played Hot, Cute, or Classically Beautiful most days, and our responses were generally the same. None of us were hot; that was an honor reserved for the girls who played club volleyball and smelled of Garnier Fructisse leave-in conditioner. The "cute" label went to Millie, the only member of our trio who hadn't yet hit five feet. Hailey and I boldly used "classically beautiful" to describe ourselves; we both had round faces and chubby knees, though that's where our Rubenesque qualities ended.

I cleared my throat. Hailey glanced up, annoyed; she was busy performing surgery on her Lunchable dessert pizza. "I'd say definitely classically beautiful," she declared, turning back to the pizza and coating it with oily chocolate frosting. Millie nodded. "That's exactly what I was gonna say," she added, tilting her head back to finish her green apple Go-Gurt. She smacked her lips, strings of bright green yogurt still dripping from her tongue. "Wait, guys, do me."

Hailey and I tilted our heads as if considering the question for the first time. "I'd say cute," Hailey said. I nodded sagely. "Yeah, that's what I was gonna say, too."

I've always deluded myself about beauty. I'm too lazy to engage with the truly transformative acids and peels and glosses; I'd rather sit back and let my friends lie to me, declaring me Classically Beautiful when the only classical thing about my looks is the Regency-era acne scarring. Grooming feels like a grueling requirement, a dreary way to spend my time. Ideally, I'd love to be hot without any of the effort. Just throw me into a torture chute where my face, hair, and nails can be shellacked into submission while I watch movies and order fireworks online.

I'm alone in this approach, at least in my immediate family. The women in my family approach grooming with the solemnity of eighteenth-century matriarchs securing advantageous marriages for their wart-covered daughters. This is because the women in my family have always worked in hair salons. When my grandmother wasn't chain-smoking, she was dishing out ill-advised perms to unfortunate clients who were too meek to say no. My mother followed in her footsteps, training as a manicurist and spending her days crammed into a salon with chemically altered customers. But the beauty gene skipped me, even after I spent nine months cooking in my mother's womb in a mixture of uterine fluid and acetone. I picture my fetal self, eyes squeezed shut in annoyance, sloshing around in her gooey abdominal cavity as she joined her fellow nail techs in screaming along to "Lovergirl" by Teena Marie. Months later, I enter the world screaming, unkempt, and undeniably fuzzy.

Fuzzy. That's a good way to put it. My body hair is blond and surprisingly minimal, but I was preternaturally blessed in the facial hair arena. By the time I hit fifth grade, my eyebrows had knitted themselves together in a near-complete unibrow. The hint of a mustache grew more pronounced as I advanced toward puberty. Fortunately, my mom had access to an unlimited supply of facial wax. She also moved in a social circle full of sadistic cosmetologists who knew God's truth: that, if you spend enough time in a salon, there are endless ways to alter your appearance. This was especially true in the early 2000s, the age of skinny string-bean eyebrows and thick, chalky highlights. If you ran out of ways to alter yourself, you obviously weren't thinking creatively enough. It's because of this influence—as well as my mother's tendency to stare at my face and point out the exact number of stray hairs beneath my eyebrows—that I ended up waxed beyond recognition, with approximately five eyebrow hairs to my name by the time I graduated from high school.

Now, just shy of thirty, my eyebrows still haven't grown back. In fact, a few more soldiers have fallen, which is a problem in this age of the lush natural brow. There's certainly an argument to be made here about the lifelong consequences of the way we alter ourselves during girlhood. I'd scrutinize that, but I'm too busy Photoshopping Gilbert Gottfried's head onto Ashlee Simpson's body.

My issues with grooming extend to skin care. I've had horrible skin since the day I got my period at eleven, a fateful day that started with me clutching one sore tit and ended with me curled up on the couch, heating pad across my abdomen, gleefully skipping taekwondo class while also worrying that the neighborhood dogs could smell my crotch. The next day, I awoke with the pores of a teenager. My forehead was caked with unsightly red bumps, my nose was dotted with blackheads, and my cheeks looked like an oil slick. I was a pubescent Yellowstone, covered in geysers of pus that threatened to spew out of my face every hour on the hour. Meanwhile, most of my peers had yet to ride the crimson wave, leaving them with smooth alabaster skin. They were cherubs (cute), and I was Sloth from *The Goonies* (classically beautiful).

Enter Proactiv, a barbaric skin care system developed in 1995. Proactiv's three-step system is the marauding Viking horde of the skincare industry, promising to annihilate every inch of bacteria—good and bad—from your tween face. First, you scrub with a cleanser full of scratchy microbeads. You follow that with a toner that I can only assume is made of pure gasoline and, when used daily, makes your face peel like a clementine. The final step is a so-called moisturizer with a warning label similar to that of rat poison.

Proactiv didn't work against my genetically doomed skin. My face got redder, blotchier, and pimplier by the day. Desperate for a solution, I pummeled my face with St. Ives Apricot Scrub, creating a series of invisible wounds across my cheeks. After that, I tortured myself with Noxzema pads, screaming in the bathroom as acid seeped into my pores. I finished my regimen with a bright orange CoverGirl foundation, which I poured into my palm and slapped on like aftershave.

Nothing worked. As I write this, my pores still gape like a coral reef despite my marginally improved relationship to facial cleansing. My only consolation is the knowledge that, should the earth descend into *Mad Max*–style water wars, I'll avoid the evil overlords' breeding harems. They'll take one look at me, scream at my overflowing sebum stores, and send me straight to the labor camps. There, I'll be free to hang out and gossip.

I've made several attempts to engage with the beauty industry. I got my hands on a plastic tub of loose face powder sometime in junior high. I used my mom's fluffy kabuki brush to apply the powder to my eyelids, eyebrows, lips, and T-zone, leaving behind a matte, crusty expression like that of a dehydrated Gila monster. I stared at myself in the mirror and whispered: "*Glamour.*"

In high school, I became obsessed with eliminating my dark, shadowy under-eye circles. They're purple and permanent, my only visible inheritance from my dad's weary Texan bloodline. I caked on liquid concealer three shades too light for my complexion and walked from class to class with reverse raccoon eyes. Later, in college, I learned to curl my hair and administer thick globs of stolen

Sephora lipstick, painting on layer after layer until my lips stuck out an extra half inch. Nothing felt right. Each attempt at glitz felt more clownish than the last. I was too fussy for fake eyelashes, too impatient to let my nails dry, and too heavy-handed for the stark facial contouring of the early 2010s. Even when I managed to paint on the face of an angel, I had the heart of a gerbil, nose twitching nervously as I scouted out the nearest bathroom and prayed for distraction in the form of a tasty pellet.

Now, here I am, at a time when the beauty industry is clearly out of ideas. Gone are the days of under-eye circles and shiny T-zones; the cosmetic companies have been forced to move with the times, thus inventing an entirely new crop of imperfections to target. Women have to be kept on our *toes*. God forbid we revolt and leave the house with visible pores.

If the magazines are to be believed, I need an expensive prescription lotion to treat my bumpy arms. I need to wash my hair daily with a detoxifying shampoo. No, wait—I need to forgo washing my hair *entirely*, relying instead on the cleansing powers of cheap cooking oil. I need a twelve-step skin care routine that requires navigating an arcane Excel sheet and costs $475. Most pressing, I need regular full-body chemical peels to remedy a mysterious and potentially terminal condition known as Strawberry Legs.

It's too much. It's too much for me; it's even too much for the women in my mom's nail salon. They've all used the same shade of red nail lacquer and blue eye shadow for decades, confidently sticking with the beauty standards of the early 1980s. I haven't visited my grandmother's hair salon since she died, but if I had to guess, the clientele hasn't aged a bit. I imagine them still sitting under fire-hazard dome hair dryers, perfectly preserved in formaldehyde and perm solution, methodically massaging Pond's Cold Cream into their necks.

That's not to say that the salon biddies have it all figured out. Of those that are still living, most have hacking coughs from years of inhaling hairspray and dusting themselves with talc-filled powder puffs. But in keeping with outdated beauty regimens, these broads have managed to thwart the most sinister lie of the beauty industry: that decay is preventable if one simply *buys another product*. That lie demands trading in your Pond's Cold Cream—a multipurpose, utilitarian product—for a string of mysterious serums and oils and masks and creams.

The mysterious serums and oils and masks and creams will not work for the salon biddies. They decay by the day. They look rough. I look rough. *We all look rough*, and spending an extra ten grand over one's lifetime will not delay that inevitability. Best-case scenario, buying into the beauty industry will only slightly reduce the number of crevices that promise to form across my eyelids once I hit fifty.

Better to lie to myself, I think. Better to gnaw on Bosco Sticks with an unhinged vigor, forcing my friends to classify me as Hot, Cute, or Classically Beautiful. *You are none of those things*, they'll say, shaking their heads in annoyance. *And all*. The words are as meaningless as the cosmetic labels that dance across my email in-box like a parade of mean little sugar plum fairies. The definitions of Hot, Cute, and Classically Beautiful change by the day, dictated solely by whether someone at Estée Lauder is grinding for a holiday bonus. "Mama needs a vacation house in the Poconos," some executive might gleefully whisper, launching a new trend that involves shaving one's head and stapling a series of Medusa-inspired eels to one's scalp. I'd rather hide in my mother's massaging pedicure chair, clinging to my self-proclaimed Classically Beautiful status and deleting any marketing emails that dare suggest otherwise. I can't afford the alternative.

Out of Office

The corporate man's urine stream is stronger than most. It's a powerful current driven by bad Keurig coffees and Big Gulps full of Diet Coke, the product of uncanny kidney function that somehow smacks of sexism. Sonically, it is unmuffleable. No amount of restroom insulation can spare an unfortunate employee the indignity of hearing one's male boss piss out a big one. I know this firsthand, having spent many hours hunched at an office-issued computer, fingers frozen over the keyboard, wide-eyed and staring at a blank spot on my desk, listening to my employer's fifth high-octane pee of the day.

It didn't help that the bathroom echoed. The whole place echoed. The office was one large, tile-floored room, churchlike in its silence save for the occasional throat-clearing or distant car horn. On one side of the office was a hallway, where stylish architects from the firm upstairs strutted out for coffee multiple times a day. On the other side was a leather-working shop owned by a nice bearded man. In the middle was our office, approximately two hundred square feet and designed like a laboratory observation box for rats with polio. There wasn't a textile in sight, so even the most subtle whisper ricocheted across the room. Ordinary board meetings took on the tone of a horde of Vikings running screaming toward Valhalla. I could not listen to podcasts for fear that the sound would escape my headphones, revealing my Bigfoot obsession to my esteemed colleagues. Amid all of this was the bathroom, located about six paces from my desk, where I sat pretending to know how to do my job.

This was my second job out of college, a nonprofit mishmash with a list of responsibilities ranging from pithy tweeting to watering the office plants. I did not volunteer to water the office plants, but I was the youngest member of staff, and a girl, and I had one large tattoo that occasionally peeked out of my tasteful Banana Republic outlet blouses. These qualities, my boss reasoned, doomed me to carry out horticultural responsibilities that lay far outside of my job description.

The plants were few and far between, a feeble attempt to liven up a space more sterile than a gynecologist's office. At least gynecologist's offices have magazines; this office was glass-walled and austere, the reading material limited to a pile of glossy pamphlets. Sometimes, one of the pamphlets would slide off the pile, at which point my boss would frown, stride purposefully to the pamphlet table, shift the wayward pamphlet back into place with a curt nod, then stride purposefully back to his desk to type extremely loudly. He did a lot of purposeful striding. He was a busy man, one who took many calls and scheduled hours-long citadels with other men of business, each of whom boasted a more powerful urine stream than the next.

I never could figure out what he did all day, although it certainly seemed important. That's why I was surprised when he found the time to haul two giant peace lilies into the office. Earlier that week, a local shop owner had paid our office a visit. "We need to liven this place up a bit," she noted, running a finger along an empty particleboard bookshelf. "Maybe some plants."

The next day, in comes my boss with the peace lilies. He strode purposefully through the door and dropped the plants near my desk without a word. He then strode purposefully back to his car and returned with two more peace lilies. In all, he made three purposeful trips, assembling a leafy line of six of the largest houseplants I'd ever seen. He shook the potting soil off his hands. "Here are those plants we talked about," he said before striding back to his desk.

This was the latest weirdness in a long string of weirdnesses that could only occur at a small nonprofit. At a nonprofit, no one tells you what you're supposed to be doing, but you damn well better figure it out. I knew that my boss expected me to care for the peace lilies, though he never came out and *asked*. I had expressed no interest in this responsibility. It was not in my job description. I did not know *how* to care for peace lilies. My plant knowledge was limited to one very small cactus I had purchased on a whim from Walmart.

Intimidated, I gently watered the peace lilies for a day or two until I forgot. That was a Thursday. I arrived at the office the following Monday to find the peace lilies dead, wilted on the floor like a horrible crime scene. I slunk in a few minutes after my boss, who looked at me with raised eyebrows. "Plants aren't looking so good," he scolded, annoyed with me for failing to adequately complete the task I was never asked to do. I crept over to one of the lilies and inspected it. "Maybe they just need more sunlight," I muttered, dragging one of the plants over to the large window at the front of the office. Just then, a random pedestrian with a bright red mohawk gallivanted up to the window, banged on it a few times, stuck his tongue out, and mooned me.

This is a great representation of the beginning of my professional career, which I spent staring at the wall with no clue as to what I was supposed to be doing. It started with my first job out of college, working at a quirky T-shirt shop where I was not allowed to sit down. The shop sat at the end of a crumbling commercial strip, sandwiched between a fussy Italian restaurant and a head shop with a drunken-gnome mascot. We didn't get much foot traffic, so the daily T-shirt inventory stayed exactly the same most days. I got really good at folding.

After that, I scored a gig at a small magazine in my hometown. There I learned how to size images for Facebook posts and withstood several months of quiet bullying from an office accountant who took an instant dislike to my sweater collection. "You're lucky the publisher hasn't seen that cardigan," she sniffed one day, gesturing toward my cozy knitted duster. "It looks like something from Goodwill." (It was—I made twelve dollars an hour part-time.)

The magazine world made more sense to me than the T-shirt world. At least at the magazine there was always something to do, and I could spend most of the day sitting without incurring the wrath of the beautiful Christian mural artist who supervised me at the T-shirt shop. Still, the professional confusion remained. Three months prior to my hiring, I was flashing my college classmates, tanked on frozen mango margaritas at a Tex-Mex dive called El Puente. What was I doing in an *office*?

I wasn't new to the working world. I've worked a ragtag collection of part-time jobs since I was fifteen. As soon as I got my learner's driving permit, I was paid under the table to organize Bottle Rockets at Big John's Fireworks just off the Branson highway junction. Come June, there's a fireworks stand roughly every two miles between St. Louis and Arkansas; thus, the competition was stiff, and customers were few and far between. Plus, my friend's dad owned the place, so I wasn't beholden to any expectation of professional conduct. My friend and I spent most of our time luxuriating in lawn chairs, watching eighteen-wheelers trundle by, gazing across the highway at the theater where a famed Branson magician performed nightly. "Wouldn't it be so insane if [famed magician] came to pick up some fireworks?" I asked her, leaning back in my lawn chair and lazily tearing into a Sour Punch Straw. She yawned. "There's no way," she muttered, looking the other way as two fifth-grade boys made off with half of our Sparkler inventory. Later that week, on my one day off, she sold a truckload of Roman candles to Kirby VanBurch himself. He looked like shit, she texted me, trying to ease the sting.

After that, I scored a job at a sweltering shaved-ice shack half a mile from my parents' semirural subdivision. On my first day, the owner taught me the art of shaving ice. "You want to lift with the knees, not with the back," she grunted, hoisting a slippery five-pound ice block from a cooler behind the shack. She rested the block on her giant, spray-tanned rack and brushed a few errant bleached-blond hairs back into her high ponytail. She beckoned me back into the shack, her flip-flops sticking to the syrupy floor with every step. Spent, she plunked the ice block onto the shaver, a medieval-looking device with a hand crank, and leaned back, breathing heavy. "We don't want a dense shave," she panted, pointing at the hand crank. "We want lacy, pillow snow. Y'know—delicate." I stepped up to the shaver just as she smacked a grasshopper with a paper towel roll. "Son of a bitch," she muttered, pouring a shot of banana shaved-ice syrup into a Styrofoam cup. She took a swig, then glanced outside at a red-faced little boy. He had dropped his rainbow-colored shaved ice onto the ground next to a picnic table. The owner took another sip from her syrup cup, belched gently, and looked me in the eye. "No refunds," she said, reaching into her cutoffs to scratch a mosquito bite.

So, no, the magazine wasn't my first time working for the Man. But the magazine job *was* my first time navigating the rules of adult professional engagement, an arcane system full of arbitrary demands. Take, for example, the magazine office's phone system. The office employed a glamorous part-time administrative professional, but one woman was no match for the volume of calls that pelted the phone lines starting at 7:30 a.m. every day. The entire office was expected to pitch in, dispatching calls from our desk phones like a bunch of harried switchboard operators. I learned about the policy during my first week in the office, when a loud woman from the ad sales department came up behind me, gave me a dead-eyed smile, and squeezed my shoulders, digging her square-cut French manicure into my skin. "Answering the phone is everyone's responsibility," she whispered. "That means you, too." I soon learned that the office phone was never allowed to ring more than twice. If it did, the French-manicured saleswoman would slam her hands on her desk and yell "PHONE!" until someone picked up the call.

This is how I entered the professional realm: anxious, confused, and convinced that the rules of engagement were impossible to follow. Should I eat lunch at my desk to appear more committed to my tasks, or should I eat in the office common area to take a stab at networking? And what did networking entail, exactly? As far as I could tell, it involved standing in a stiff shirt, pasting a smile on your face, and nodding as the men around you drink light beer and say insane things. Later, you email them to let them know how much you enjoyed listening to them say insane things, and wouldn't they like to say more insane things to you over a coffee sometime? This is how professional connections are made.

Networking isn't socializing, per se—professional socialization is something else entirely. At the magazine, socializing involved a cutthroat Halloween photo shoot where readers were asked to vote for their favorite Halloween costumes. *Halloween!* I thought. *Now, this, I can handle.* Little did I know I was among a group of professionals with the competitive spirit of a herd of hyenas fighting for the last wildebeest on earth. The morning of the photo shoot, my supervisor showed up in an elaborate homemade unicorn costume, complete with a glittering horn. Another work friend had stayed up all night creating an astronaut costume out of tin foil. Still another had encased herself in a massive homemade SpongeBob costume made of papier-mâché. I had painted my face, strapped on an old blue swim cap, and shown up as a member of Blue Man Group. It remains my best Halloween costume to date; it just wasn't a match for the magazine's competitive spirit.

I quit four months later, unable to crack the office culture. It made me a nervous wreck, this feeling that everyone was waiting for me to break one of the unspoken rules of grown-up work. It was all-encompassing, including everything from the phone system to kitchen etiquette to wardrobe expectations to the fact that we were apparently supposed to pay for coffee creamer, though no one ever did. It was all too vague, leaving me feeling like an immature alien surrounded by people who had somehow sprang out of the womb ready to sit at a desk for nine hours a day. Minutes before clocking out on my last day, I managed to smash a giant pilsner glass full of ice water, sending glass shards and four hundred milliliters of water spilling across my desk tsunami-style. The French-manicured saleswoman sprang up from her desk. I pictured her leaping over cubicles, pushing onlookers out of the way in an attempt to save my desk phone. Instead, she just crossed her arms tightly and shook her head.

Two weeks later, I was in the echoey glass office listening to my new boss unload a thick piss. I'd taken a job at the nonprofit hoping the rules of professionalism would come more naturally on a smaller team. They did not; they were blurrier. In the nonprofit realm, there's no handbook; there's just The Way Things Are. Dedicated nonprofit employees often keep their jobs for decades, which is great—unless you're a newcomer waiting for someone to show you the ropes. In my experience, nonprofit veterans become so accustomed to The Way Things Are that they tend to assume newcomers' brains are already equipped with a working knowledge of decades-old organizational practices.

My boss, for example, knew the entire municipal phone directory by heart. "Can you get Dan on the phone?" he asked once, flipping distractedly through a stack of documents that, for all I knew, were completely blank. "Which Dan?" I asked innocently, phone-dialing fingers at the ready. There were many Dans. There was Dan the part-time glass recycling professional. There was Dan with the bike rental program. There was Dan at the radio station that sponsored the annual Christmas parade. There was Dan the curmudgeonly Air Force veteran who volunteered at the food festival and made lascivious comments about my legs.

My boss paused and glanced up at me, incredulous. "Glass recycling Dan."

Ah, yes. *That* Dan.

The nonprofit gig was the most confusing job I've ever had. There were no spoken rules, only expectations disguised as traditions that held the organization upright like a scorpion encased in amber. The expectations always took me by surprise—for example, the time I tried to clock out for Christmas. It was 5 p.m. the day before Christmas Eve, a Wednesday, and I had loaded up my messenger bag and said my goodbyes. "See everyone Monday!" I announced, heading toward the door. My boss looked startled and shook his head slightly. "Oh," he stuttered. "Were you planning on taking Friday off?"

"Y-yes?" I asked, assuming that no one would require a nonprofit community development organization's nebulous services the day after Christmas. There would be no festivals to organize, no developers to empower, no free public parking to tweet about. My boss did not understand this.

"We're always open the day after Christmas," he said. "People have come to expect this from us."

Not one to argue, I reported to the office the day after Christmas, the building deserted save for my boss, who looked exactly the same as he always did save for a jaunty Charlie Brown Christmas tie. We sat in silence for eight hours, without a single call or email coming in or going out.

Halfway through the day, I crept to my boss's desk and presented him with a gift: a delicious tin of homemade Christmas fudge. He nodded heartily and accepted the fudge without opening it, inexplicably sniffing the outside of the tin. "Smells great," he said before placing the tin on a bookshelf near his desk. After that, I kept an eye on the tin. It never moved from its spot on the bookshelf, which told me one of two things: Either my boss was removing the fudge incredibly carefully so as not to shift the tin, or he had never opened the tin at all. One day, as he stepped out to take one of his many purposeful calls, I crept over to the shelf and peeked inside the tin. It was as I suspected: My boss had not even bothered to touch his Christmas fudge. I looked around the empty office and took a piece. Then I took another piece. I spent the next two months secretly extracting one piece of fudge a day until the tin was empty. It remained in exactly the same spot, surrounded by a halo of dust, as I filed my letter of resignation. For all I know, it's still there, waiting for someone to open it up, show it to the world, and jump into a lake in utter bafflement.

The more time I spend in the professional realm, the more I realize that it's meant to be confusing. Consider the idea of "business casual attire." As far as I can tell, the term "business casual" encompasses everything from stiff button-down blouses to turtleneck-tank top hybrids to tasteful summer sandals designed to appeal to the evil stepmother in *The Parent Trap*. Then there's that most sinister symbol of office footwear: the ballet flat.

Ballet flats are a special style of footwear, uniquely capable of absorbing one's toe stank. Wear them for a few months and they'll lose their shape, crumbling into a smushed slipper with a flattened back heel and a thick, flaking layer of dirt in the footbed. I acquired my first pair of ballet flats in high school, days before a debate tournament. While my cooler peers ran cross country and went on dates and argued over Homecoming dance themes, I squeezed myself into professional attire and prepared to waddle across a junior high cafeteria and scream about the ethical implications of commercial space travel. The flats were an unappealing shade of copper, with glittery metallic flecks that drew the eye to my plodding gait. Heels are meant to elongate the leg, but ballet flats have the opposite effect. They force your arches into an unnaturally horizontal position, turning your toes out like duck feet, erasing any hint of an ankle and creating the illusion that your calves take a hard ninety-degree turn once they hit the floor. Flats also tend to expose the roots of one's toes, creating an obscene half-moon of little ass cracks. This was the first impression I gave as I strode into my first high school debate tournament—feet jammed into flats, butt jammed into unforgiving nylon pants, the whole of my personality jammed into a scratchy two-piece ensemble from the Macy's Petites clearance rack. The picture of professionalism.

To this day, I still feel uncomfortable in business attire. I once spent a whole paycheck on Zara workwear, springing for a few lacy blouses to pair with the cheapest work pants I could find. Zipping myself into a professional ensemble feels about as natural as zipping myself into a scuba suit. A power suit doesn't make me feel like a woman of business and enterprise; it makes me feel like two toddlers stacked in a trench coat.

I'm still weirded out by the working world. The codes of professionalism are ludicrous and impossible to navigate, having been set by white dudes who walk with purpose and expect others to bend to their outdated expectations. They buy the plants, establish the work hours, and wrinkle their brows with consternation when their underlings fail to comply. It's a system designed to exclude, one that makes newcomers feel embarrassed for not immediately knowing the law of the land. Unless, naturally, you're the kind of person professionalism was designed for—a person who strides purposefully from place to place, carves their fingernails into perfectly square French manicures, and urinates publicly with abandon.

Young people are shepherded from classroom desk to cubicle desk, taught to valorize the kind of work that buries any lingering personality beneath an encyclopedic email signature. Uncertainty is addressed with corporate jargon; tattoos are covered with cardigans; humor is replaced with exaggerated Slack reactions. (Be wary of workplaces that welcome tattoos and humor; if you're truly encouraged to be yourself, there's a good chance you'll be underpaid for the privilege. Because these workplaces aren't just your employers—they're *family*.) Vacations or parental leave or side projects are, it goes without saying, never one's priority. To admit to personal aspirations outside the workplace is to invite suspicion from the square-manicured keepers of the status quo. Why would anyone want to do anything other than show up on time and listen cheerfully as their boss unleashes a thunderous piss? Who would dare imagine an existence outside of this one, where you're expected to quietly contribute to your 401(k) in the hopes that you'll be able to retire before your geriatric brain forgets that you ever had a personality at all?

When I quit my nonprofit job to write full-time, the cash trickled in at unpredictable intervals. To keep my bills paid, I picked up a few shifts at a movie theater near my apartment. It was, without a doubt, the best job I've ever had. The hours were flexible; the boss was cool. My coworkers were geniuses, a collective encyclopedia of obscure cinematic knowledge that knocked my socks off. We unclogged toilets and extracted crumpled Kleenex from the auditorium seats after each showing. We ate day-old popcorn by the fistful and gossiped about which regulars were spotted holding hands during the Sunday matinee screening. I learned to operate the digital projector, the kind of technical skill that gave me greater satisfaction than any of the work I'd done sitting in a cubicle. I was pleased with my work, and even more pleased with the discount Kit-Kats.

A few months into my tenure, my old boss stopped in for an evening showing. I was running the popcorn machine, dumping buttery kernels into the red-hot popper and giving it a hearty jiggle to reduce the risk of burnt corn. He cocked his head at me as I stepped away from the popper to ring up his concessions. He squinted with a look of mild concern, asking: "What's going *on* with you?" He couldn't fathom the idea that I might be happier popping popcorn than trying to navigate a professional realm that made me feel like E.T.

I shrugged and replied: "I'm popping popcorn." I handed him an extra-large Diet Coke and pointed him toward Theater 2.

I did return to a desk job, eventually. I spent a few years puttering around the freelance world, begging editors for scraps and driving like I had beagles strapped to my bumpers for fear of catching an ER bill. I wrote 650-word blog posts for a steel tank manufacturer. I made myself indispensable to the nation's leading trucking magazine. By the time I returned to a full-time office gig, I still hadn't figured out the ins and outs of professionalism. Lucky for me, I wound up in a more casual setting where my coworkers were just as likely to crack fart jokes as rant about the keyboard shortcut for em dashes.

It's about then that I decided to ditch the pursuit of professionalism entirely. That's not to say that I'm some kind of renegade employee. I'm not out here sprinting topless up and down the stairwell in an attempt to prove a point about sexism in the professional realm. I'm good at my job. I know what's expected of me, because my boss tells me. I treat my coworkers with kindness and humor, and they return the favor. I water my own plants—no one else's.

At the same time, I acknowledge that there will always be stuffy bosses who walk with purpose and people who can't fathom the idea of popcorn popping as a satisfying livelihood. There will always be confusing rules of engagement, especially when those rules are designed with exclusion in mind. It's easy to get caught up in the nebulous expectations of the professional realm. If you're not careful, you'll end up like me: tortured by unspoken rules, absolutely beefing the office Halloween costume contest, and permanently unable to read the room. But please—don't quit your day job. Jobs are bad—anything that stands in the way of my true calling (founder of a utopian gardening commune) is a no for me—but bills are bills.

The only way to navigate that system is to acknowledge the wholeness of your being outside of work. Even my status as a professional armpit joke writer shouldn't define me. Working in a so-called creative field doesn't change the fact that I write to make other people money—people who, no offense to my publisher, probably wouldn't care if I died in a tragic peace-lily accident tomorrow. The work is no more glamorous than my work as a popcorn popper. It's all just *work*. When you realize that, you've learned the most important thing: that the rules of the professional realm don't matter. If you, like me, still have to live by those rules from nine to five every day, just make sure to slip your feet out of your putrid ballet flats every once in a while. They're murder on the arches.

Opinion Machine

No shark movie is complete without the Knee Shot. It's the gnarliest shot of the film, captured immediately after the shark goes in for a hearty bit o' leg. One minute, an unsuspecting marine professional is enjoying a tranquil day on the water, dangling their well-muscled calves into the gentle waves; the next, they're flopping around on the dock, clutching their thigh and screaming, "MY LEG, GOOD CHRIST, MY LEG!!!!!!!!!!!!!!!!"

Pan to the Knee Shot: a gory take showing the victim's half-devoured leg, severed savagely at the knee. It's always the knee, which suggests one of two things: Either sharks don't like thigh meat, or oceanic horror films have unusually low prosthetic budgets. Either way, the viewer is treated to an uneven mess of bloody tissue and gristle, a bright sliver of bone protruding from the chomp zone. It's at this point that I sink deeper into the couch, grab a handful of Raisinettes, and absentmindedly stroke my own knee. If I'm among friends, I'll pause the movie and point to the screen to acknowledge the cinema of it all. "GREAT KNEE SHOT," I'll bellow, strings of spitty chocolate stretched between my molars.

I hardly ever watch shark movies among friends. For me,

shark cinema is a solitary pursuit, like buffing my calloused feet or scream-singing to Tori Amos. Shark movies are for Sunday nights, that blessed window of time after I've roasted the week's cauliflower and walked the dog and Windexed the crapper. Shark movies are my weekend vice of choice, a supreme indulgence of my baser instincts. They're inevitably very bad movies, perfect for curling up to consume a box of Bomb Pops with the fervor of a lifelong chainsmoker. They're formulaic and easy to follow, which makes them ideal background noise for painting my toenails or applying my acidic body lotion that burns like hellfire. My Sunday night beauty routine, questionable in its efficacy, varies—but the shark movies are a must.

The shark movie habit is relatively recent, though I've always been gleefully horrified by sharks as a concept. As a kid, I tiptoed into the elementary school library to peruse an illustrated Eyewitness book called *Shark*. The book promised to demystify the "fascinating world of sharks," outlining "their behavior and secret underwater lives." I opened the book, flipping to a random page. I took one look at the header photo—a seven-foot replica of a megalodon shark jaw—and slammed the book closed with a hearty *nnnnno*.

To marine biologists, sharks are a direct link to primeval predators, a supreme source of evolutionary data. To me, they're proof that God doesn't exist. If He did, he'd have zapped those sons of bitches with His mighty laser pointer long ago. You're telling me that 70 percent of earth's planetary surface is swimming with four-thousand-pound predators? You're telling me those four-thousand-pound predators have an average of fifteen rows of teeth in each jaw? You're telling me that surfers—arguably the most beautiful people *on earth*—are paddling directly into *shark-infested waters* to catch a sweet wave when they should be spending their time asking me on a *romantic breakfast date*? Talk about begging for a Knee Shot.

Shark movies drive home an inconvenient truth: that humans

have no business hanging out in the ocean's briny depths. "But, Lillian," you say, hopping out of your open-top Jeep to wax your sick board. "The ocean is full of rich ecological evidence and groundbreaking scientific data."

Okay? It's also full of fish that look like the literal Devil.

"But Lillian," you say. "Sharks aren't *bad*—they're just doing what they've evolved to do over millennia."

Okay??? If your neighbor had spent thousands of years evolving into a megapredator, would you stroll into their living room wearing nothing but a genital-hugging wet suit?

That's the other reason I like shark movies. They're proof that my fear of the ocean is perfectly practical. If anything, they lend me a sense of superiority because I wouldn't be caught dead in a shark's living room. Actually, that's how I feel about all horror movies. Take the Alien film franchise, which begins when sex astronaut Sigourney Weaver ventures into space, a famously hostile realm, and then has the *gall* to be surprised when a parasitic extraterrestrial bursts out of her friend's torso. Take *The Descent*, in which a group of gals with incredible collective upper-body strength decide to shimmy into an unexplored cave system, which is—surprise!—inhabited by bloodthirsty humanoid creatures. Take *The Exorcist*, in which a curious Catholic priest and recreational archaeologist unearths an artifact representing the ancient demon Pazuzu, which incites all manner of hellish, projectile-vomit-tinged mayhem. Fools. *FOOLS!!!*

If I were a more intelligent woman, I'd try to parse my interest in these movies. I wonder: What does it say about me as a person? Maybe it says something about the way I like to master villains and scary things, keeping them trapped in my television. Maybe it says I am gross and bad. More than anything, I think it just speaks to the fact that I like to turn my brain off.

Shark movies are objectively bad media, which is my favorite way to reward myself for a difficult week. I'm not entirely without taste; I need my objectively bad media to fit at least one of the following criteria:

- Someone gets their leg chomped off
- Someone gets their Achilles heel slashed
- Someone falls in love with someone else—but that person has a *secret*
- Someone falls in love with someone else who either chops their leg or Achilles off
- Someone, at some point, undergoes a makeover montage and steps out in a purple tube dress

For me, there is no greater pleasure than viewing objectively bad media. That pleasure extends to other things that don't require the use of my brain. I like pop music that makes me want to swing my little boobs around. I like a Taco Bell bean burrito with no sauce and extra onions, which I eat in my car using a patented bean extraction method I've dubbed the Burrito Suck. I drink a lot of gas station coffee, which has an immediate and violent effect on my large intestine. Actually, gas station coffee is probably the closest I'll ever get to the thrill of the Wild West. Every time I get my 7-Eleven breakfast blend, I feel a kinship with an imaginary band of gold prospectors, drinking their coffee out of metal pails and squabbling over who gets the last piece of hardtack before they all die from infected hangnails.

All these things could reasonably be classified as "guilty pleasures." If my Twitter feed is to be believed, now is the time to reclaim guilty pleasures. Objectively bad movies are heralded as bastions of cinema. ("What you do MEAN you've never seen *Freddy Got Fingered*?") Self-indulgent beauty rituals are essential self-care. Using your fingernail to scrape queso from a slow cooker is a revolutionary feminist act. If you ask me, it's all a natural reaction to the dawn of the social media age, which demands that we signpost our interests with the flair of a Macy's Christmas display.

It started with Xanga, arguably the first website that allowed users to communicate their Billie Joe Armstrong fandom via rudimentary HTML. MySpace came shortly after, with more robust personalization options and a worryingly large reach. But MySpace's personalization options were meager compared to Facebook, which offered users the chance to broadcast their entire personhood through Likes, Groups, and Pieces of Flair.

I was allowed a Facebook account at thirteen. I was thrilled, ready to create an entirely new persona based on carefully selected Likes and a perfectly penned Bio. With a flick of the wrist, I could put my curated foot forward, broadcasting myself as someone who liked Band of Horses and the Pigeon Detectives and *Monty Python's Flying Circus*, all hallmarks of the coolest of cool. With a well-placed emoticon, I could establish myself as the lighthearted class clown; with a series of ellipses, I could declare myself the poet of ninth grade.

I began the overwhelming task of uploading my entire self onto social media. I spent hours building my profile, attempting to upload my entirety onto my new Facebook page. When I say "entirety," I mean just the cool stuff. Developing my Internet Self was an exercise in scientific selection, of cross-pollinating my own vague interests with the interests of my much cooler peers to create a digital avatar that publicly liked all the right things. Every band I followed, every Facebook group I joined, every status update I posted from my parents' dusty Dell computer, every Like I administered was by design. I moved with intention, careful and cunning, scheming up an entire personality from scratch.

I acknowledge this as troubling behavior, but I was thirteen. My brain had barely begun growing. Today I hope to lend slightly more authenticity to my online interactions. Still, I fear that I've uploaded so much of myself onto Perez Hilton's internet that it feels impossible to extricate my value from my public persona. In the Xanga days, I could've proclaimed my love for shark movies to my three subscribers, who each would've responded with some variation of "rawr xD." Today, if I dare to tweet an earnest observation about a particularly cinematic Knee Shot, I risk inviting replies that call my character into question. I imagine they'd look something like this:

> I'm glad you enjoyed *Reef of Pain*, but that film set sharks back at least 25 years—which you'd know if you bothered to learn about aquatic ecosystems.
>
> —@reefdoctor

> kind of interesting that you can enjoy shark movies when there are hundreds, perhaps millions, of children actively in danger of being eaten by a shark as we speak??
>
> —@ItsAlexaActually

> Really devastating how we've lost touch with true cinema.
>
> —@JoyceCarolOates

> bro joyce carol oates hates you lmao
>
> —@theworldneedsursmile

> omg imagine getting owned by joyce carol oates couldn't be me
>
> —@slutforcandycorn

> DM TO PROMOTE
>
> —@00000piss

Best-case scenario, I get ten Likes on the tweet and move on. Worst-case scenario, a stranger reports me to the National Fish and Wildlife Foundation and Joyce Carol Oates puts me on blast for having bad taste in film. The entire world seems poised to assign sociopolitical value to my stupidest takes, assuming the very worst about me, someone they will never, ever meet.[*]

Thus, the pressure to be publicly infallible. If my entire self is available for global condemnation, my most mundane interests must *also* be publicly infallible. More than that: They must be deep, meaningful, and worthy of scholarly defense. Somehow, the argument to *just let people enjoy things* has been twisted into "all enjoyable things are worth valorizing on the Internet." If we have to live our entire lives in the public sphere, we'd want to make an argument for *Reef of Pain* as peak revolutionary cinema, wouldn't we? Everything we do, everything we enjoy, has to send a message: This is who I *am*.

I like to think I've always had bad taste, but I've only recently become tempted to defend it as some sort of innate intellectualism. I used to like things for the sake of liking them—when I became aware of boy bands as a concept, for example. I was seven, sitting cross-legged in front of my family's gigantic box of a television—one of those four-hundred-pound 1999 models with a bulbous two-foot cord enclosure jutting out of the back. I knew it would squish me like a bug if it toppled over, but that didn't stop me from scooting as close to the screen as possible. I can't remember what Disney Channel show I was watching, but I was rapt. The commercials were even better than the actual programming. If you were lucky, you'd see the girl from *7th Heaven* talk about what the American flag means to her. If you were luckier, you'd see a music video. I had tuned in just in time to catch the latter, the title song for *Inspector Gadget*, which came out in 1999.

The movie looked fine—as far as I could tell, Matthew Broderick starred as a man who could light a cigarette with his thumb—but this music video was incredible. The title song, "I'll Be Your Every-

---

[*] Do not misunderstand me: Some people deserve to be blasted for bad takes. If you post something hateful, bigoted, or otherwise mean-spirited, I wish you an eternity of hot, spiky, quote tweets. Please, conservative pundits, read this and know: I pray for your digital silence.

thing," was performed by a boy band called Youngstown. The band was short-lived, dissolving shortly after releasing a sophomore album titled *Down for the Get Down*. In that moment, they were the most beautiful thing I had ever seen. I moved closer to the screen, focusing on the Technicolor pixels that swam around the singer's chin piercing.

I was speechless. Each member of Youngstown wore baggy cargo pants, just a hair north of JNCOs. They danced in perfect harmony, swinging their arms and hips in a manner that I had never seen before. As they jiggled their tiny bottoms, I felt an unfamiliar sensation brewing in my belly: the divine anguish of obsession. I had to have more boy bands or I would die.

Thus began my initial spiral into bad taste. I quickly moved on to the big guns, dabbling in Backstreet Boys fandom before landing on *NSYNC. I'd like to say that I liked *NSYNC because of their soulful lyrics or stylin' moves; in reality, I was just transfixed by Justin Timberlake's curly, curly head. In my eyes, he was leagues above the other members of the band. Lance was blond in a way that I find unsettling to this day. J.C. was handsome, but nondescript, like the state of Oklahoma. Joey was the unsexy kind of Italian, and Chris looked like Andy Serkis. But Justin moved me to obsession from day one.

I suspect lack of access had something to do with it. I couldn't participate in the band's global fandom. We didn't have a computer, my Walkman was unreliable, and there was no way I'd ever see Justin in concert. (Boy bands didn't come to my Missouri hometown, although Christian boy bands did.) *NSYNC was inaccessible save for the CD that I played round the clock on my purple boom box. To know they were *out there*? Just *living*? Wearing outfits and flying on airplanes and yielding at stop signs and KISSING OTHER GIRLS? It *tortured* me.

It was also the most fun I've ever had. I begged for *NSYNC school supplies. I saved up my quarters and purchased an *NSYNC poster from the Scholastic Book Fair. I didn't understand what was happening to me; all I knew was that it felt violent, painful, and completely, incandescently blissful.

I'd love to feel that feeling—that deep, torturous, all-consuming obsession—again. I've certainly had other passions. I got into horses, along with every other ten-year-old in the Ozarks. I spent my tween years reading fantasy novels over and over again until the pages turned yellow and the spines withered. I burned a lot of CDs, venturing to Walmart for a giant pile of crystal discs that came with their own colorful paper sleeves. As recently as last year, I nursed a brief fixation on the American West.

But I can't remember the last time I felt the giddy thrill of girlish obsession. I suppose it could be a natural consequence of getting older and realizing that the rent must be paid and the car must be washed and the work must be done, which leaves very little time to meditate on Justin Timberlake's favorite color. (It's baby blue.) But I suspect it's also a consequence of living life under scrutiny. I feel this undeniable pressure to be an Opinion Machine. By existing on social media, I've made my life available for public consumption in a way that I couldn't fathom in 2001. Anyway, at that point, I was too busy constructing a Barbie stage out of Lincoln Logs. (My parents would not buy me the *NSYNC marionette dolls sold in stores at the time; instead, I pranced my Barbies across the stage and made them gossip about the band. "DO YOU THINK CHRIS IS HANDSOME," Millennium Princess Barbie screamed. Surfer Barbie replied: "NO ARE YOU SERIOUS HE LOOKS LIKE ANDY SERKIS.")

To survive in an intensely public world is to be comfortable with scrubbing away your nuance, flattening your identity into a one-dimensional slab of pixels compact enough to send flying through cyberspace and into the clutches of data farmers. There's this endless pressure to get everything right, from the way you communicate your interests to the way you engage with Julia Fox's latest crotch antics. Now, instead of fretting over which Green Day song to attach to our MySpace profiles, we fret over whether or not we need to comment on the news of the day, knowing that we are, by and large, a bunch of perfect idiots with no business commenting on anything at all. We're performing personality in an endless public forum designed to open up our tender underbellies for everyone else's consumption. Everything is a part of your personal brand. *Don't* mess it up.

Shark movies are my way of grappling with all of this. I don't need to proclaim the value of these guilty pleasures; they're just bad movies that I enjoy watching. They have no bearing on my character. Watching them is not a feminist act. I'm not so self-satisfied to call this a revolutionary approach; it might even be a regressive one. I just don't want to assign political value to every single choice I make. At least, not publicly.

I should say: This is new for me. I was caught up in publicly signposting my personality for years, cherry-picking interests with my peers' perceptions in mind. I squirmed over music, movies, and clothing with external validation and imagined moral value in mind, feeling pressure to send a *message* with every selection I made. It's the natural consequence of my people-pleasing tendencies. If every single choice has direct bearing on my value as a human being, how can I be expected to make any choices at all?

Yes, it's hard to cultivate intellectual independence under the influence of social media—but we're not entirely without agency. We aren't babies moving through the world grabbing colorful plastic keys, motivated only by immediate sensory satisfaction. We can choose to avoid media we find objectionable or harmful. We can also simply consume media in private, choosing never to speak of it again. Take it from someone who spent her early twenties working through an obscure horror blog's list of The Most Disturbing Films Ever Made. Watched 'em. Not gonna talk about 'em. *No one has to know.*

Not long ago, I watched a new shark flick. It starred Alicia Silverstone, whom I love because she has the chin of a teenager. She is also, I found out, a very unconvincing screamer—another requirement for my preferred shark media. In the movie, Alicia ventures to a remote waterfront resort with her husband, who feels weird about Alicia's recent miscarriage. What follows is a clumsy attempt to address marital trauma in between shark attacks. I watched it while applying my acidic body lotion, yowling in pain as Alicia tried to outswim a two-ton megapredator.

I think she dies in the end. To be honest, I don't remember. The film's plot slipped vaporlike from my ears the second the credits started to roll. I *can* confidently say this: It was very, very bad. So bad I thought about tweeting some sort of snarky limerick. I even brainstormed a few words that rhyme with *sea*. In the end, I decided it was no one's business.

Quiz: Which Boy Band Archetype Is Your Perfect Boo?

〜〜〜〜

Do you belong on the arm of the floppy-banged frontman, or would you rather spend your weekend shakin' that thang with the bad boy of the group?

Choose a color.
A. Baby blue
B. Dark, sexy maroon
C. Pretty pink
D. Slime green

What's your signature style?
A. Trendy, but not *too* trendy
B. Head-to-toe leather
C. A comfy sweatshirt and boyish bangs
D. A vintage unitard that zips down to my pubic mound. Also, inexplicable ski goggles.

Choose a personality quiz.

A. "What's Your Ultimate Summer Jam?"

B. "Which CoverGirl Lipstick Is Most Likely to Get You a Sandpapery Fingering at Homecoming?"

C. "Have You Found Your Soul Mate?"

D. "What's Your Whole . . . Deal?"

What's your after-school hobby?

A. Charming the entire Student Council

B. Writhing on a motorcycle

C. Slipping love notes into my crush's locker

D. Rigging up a complex series of antennae in an attempt to communicate with the Lost City of Atlantis

What's your role in your friend group?

A. The frontman! I'm a born leader, taking charge even when the going gets tough.

B. The naughty one. I'm not afraid to live life on the edge— especially when living on the edge involves a sandpapery fingering at Homecoming.

C. The sweetie. I'm always checking in on my pals!

D. The oddball. What can I say? No one really *gets* me.

Mostly A's: The Frontman

The boy band frontman is your perfect boo! He's the canned soup of the pop music industry: an unsophisticated choice, easily replicated, and not terribly adventurous, with eerily pristine features that'll eventually congeal into a thin layer of scum. Like canned soup, the frontman is not microwave safe; unlike canned soup, he has excellent vocal range.

Mostly B's: The Bad Boy

Okay, nasty—you're meant to be with the bad boy. He's got tiny spikes in his hair and a stunning mastery of the modern hip thrust, and while he's more interesting than the frontman, he also drives drunk.

Mostly C's: The Sweetie

You're a real softie! The sweetie is your perfect boo, with soulful blue eyes and lackluster jawline. On one hand, you'll have less competition for his affections. On the other, you run the risk of seeming Pollyannaish and dull, a simpleton with a childish view of the sensual realm.

Mostly D's: The Oddball

The Oddball takes many forms, whether he be a delicately queer-coded fashion icon, a cyberpunk, or a man who wears vests. He's the thinking woman's choice, claimed by prepubescent girls who're already seeking to set themselves apart as A Little Different. Alternatively, he's chosen by the last member of a friend group to declare their boy band crush. (Intergalactic black holes are formed when multiple members of a prepubescent friend group select the same crush. It simply is not done.) Congrats!

Bad Egg

When I die, I'd like to be placed on Willy Wonka's Eggdicator. It's tucked away in Wonka's chocolate egg room, where a cohort of immense geese lay Pomeranian-sized golden eggs. The Eggdicator sorts the good eggs from the bad, sending the duds down an ominous chute with a resounding "honk-honk." Don't bury me; don't cremate me. Chuck my corpse onto the Eggdicator and let it sort me—good egg or bad.

God, I love to be sorted. I'm drawn to tidy categorizations that strip me of the torment of choice. Virgo, socialist, Type A, extrovert, White Sox fan. Good egg, bad egg. Slapping a label on my metaphorical blouse allows me to avoid the worst of life's uncertainties. I can navigate the world via an established lens. I can go forth with the confidence of someone who's been told they're a True Autumn complexion and should thus avoid wearing blue. Doesn't matter if I like blue; the choice has been made, leaving me with a sort of lobotomized serenity.

It started in the early aughts, the golden age of magazine personality quizzes. (The golden age of other things, too—George Foreman Grills, banana clips, platform flip-flops, and anorexia.) In elementary school, I'd languish in my grandmother's hair salon, letting incendiary puffs of Aqua Net perforate my lungs as I rifled through old issues of *Highlights* or *National Geographic Kids* in search of personality quizzes. The questions were simple—"Which Color Fits Your Personality?"—but I took them seriously. Slowly, thoughtfully, I'd complete the multiple-choice quiz until I came to the end and learned my true nature. *Orange*, I'd think. *I am orange.*

Later, my more adventurous friends introduced me to top-tier sleepover contraband: their moms' back issues of *Cosmo*. (My mom subscribed only to *Southern Living*.) *Cosmo* boasted some truly filthy personality quizzes, with titles that sent my friends and me diving into our sleeping bags in embarrassment. "What Kind of Lover Are You?" my friend Cassidy read aloud, eyebrows raised mischievously. A few minutes later, she declared me a "Slow, Tantalizing Lover." I nodded solemnly, accepting my classification even though the closest I'd ever come to sexual activity was sticking my tongue through a gummy Life-Saver and making lascivious eye contact with the kid across the street.

I like personality quizzes for the same reason I like the Eggdicator: They're a sorting mechanism. It also explains why I'm drawn to dystopian fiction—Lois Lowry's *The Giver*, for example. In the book, all twelve-year-olds are slotted tidily into an occupation based on their abilities. There's no choice in the matter; the tweens are sorted by elders who claim to know best. Obviously, this system presents one or two ethical concerns. Still, it would've made seventh grade Career Day a hell of a lot less stressful.

The same goes for Harry Potter's Sorting Hat, though I'd be loath to let J. K. Rowling sort me, knowing what I know of her politics. She'd take one look at me and scream, "VAGINA, *OBVIOUSLY*!!!" But in the series, a new Hogwarts student dons the hat, which condenses the student's entire being into one of four categories: Gryffindor, Ravenclaw, Hufflepuff, or Slytherin. Students are either courageous, erudite, trustworthy, or shrewd. The Sorting Hat requires very little introspection on the students' part; they just have to sit back, relax, and allow a sentient accessory to penetrate their innermost thoughts. The *luxury* of it all.

It's no coincidence that I was drawn to dystopian fiction, Harry Potter, and *Cosmo* personality quizzes all around the same time. Like most other tweens, I was intimidated by the branching paths I saw before me. I was overwhelmed by the sheer abundance of choice and afraid of choosing wrong, whether the choice involved a pair of jeans or an after-school activity. I didn't know what kind of person I wanted to become; I wanted a dystopian overlord to tell me so I didn't have to figure it out. I was fresh out of dystopian overlords, but I did have personality quizzes. The only problem: It's easy to cheat a personality test, even if you don't mean to.

Personality tests have a finite number of outcomes, usually no more than four or five. When you take a personality test, you have an ideal outcome in mind. You know your favorite Spice Girl; you know which Lizzie McGuire hairstyle you prefer. Like J. K. Rowling's bespectacled boy wizard, you *know*—consciously or unconsciously—how you want to be sorted. More often than not, in order to achieve the results you want, you have to cheat the test. Here, let's do an example:

Which Hot Pop Song Is Your Ultimate Summer Jam?

If it's 2005, I already *know* my ultimate summer jam. It's Gwen Stefani's "Hollaback Girl." I loved Gwen Stefani, she of the cartoonish red lips, scandalous cropped sweatshirts, and genuinely mindboggling approach to cultural appropriation. If I wanted to claim "Hollaback Girl" as my ultimate summer jam, I had to navigate the test carefully. I'd have to dodge any responses that might direct me to, say, "Don't Cha" by the Pussycat Dolls. ("Don't Cha" was my mom's favorite song, so it was off the table. Besides, that song was for hotties—real maneaters. The only man I'd ever eaten was the Jolly Green Giant, peeking out from a can label accidentally baked into my corn casserole one Thanksgiving.)

With these high stakes in mind, I'd complete the test, selecting the answers that would steer me toward the result I desperately wanted. A question might look like this:

What's your goal for the summer?
A. To show the neighborhood bully who's boss
B. To leave all the boys at the neighborhood pool drooling
C. To dance until I drop

Obviously the only appropriate answer here is Option A. Option B would likely result in "Don't Cha," or maybe "My Humps" by the Black Eyed Peas. Option C could match up to any number of insipid dance tunes—Sean Paul's "We Be Burnin' " or Pretty Ricky's "Grind with Me." No, "Hollaback Girl" was the thinking woman's summer jam, making Option A the clear choice.

Was I truthful in choosing Option A? No. For one thing, I didn't have a neighborhood bully; anyway, my actual goal for the summer was to conquer my asthma. I was sick of toting my inhaler around, especially after accidentally getting a Cheeto lodged in the mouthpiece and shooting it into the back of my throat as I took a puff. But I'd do anything to fool myself that "Hollaback Girl" was, in fact, my ultimate summer jam.

Cheating the quiz likely meant cheating myself. Maybe answering the questions honestly would've unlocked something in my twelve-year-old brain, revealing some buried aspect of my truest self. Maybe I'd achieve enlightenment by accepting "We Be Burnin' " as my ultimate summer jam. At the time, it didn't matter. I wanted the personality quiz to sort me, but only in a way that puffed up my adolescent ego, affirming that I was becoming the kind of person I wanted to be.

It's the same with grown-up personality tests. The Myers-Briggs test sorts subjects into sixteen distinct personality types, some clearly preferable to others. The ISTJ type, for example, is described as "quiet, serious, practical, and matter-of-fact." Meanwhile, the ESFP type is "outgoing, friendly, and accepting—exuberant lovers of life." Oh my god! One of these types is *clearly superior.* If I'm taking this test, I'm going to do my absolute damnedest to steer my Myers-Briggs type toward the ESFP zone. I don't care if I have to lie to myself; I'm not getting thrown in with the curmudgeons.

Years after "We Be Burnin' " fell off the Top 40 charts, I pursued what is perhaps the greatest exercise in delusional self-pigeonholing: I joined a sorority. My dad still crows about his University of Oklahoma fraternity experience, which he maintains was the best time of his life. "That's when they realized we had *crapped* in the *chili*," he cackles, retelling his favorite collegiate anecdote. He'll dig up old Polaroids showing nude poker tournaments and raucous tailgate parties, tinged with the sort of debauchery one might expect from Carter-era coeds. It was *Animal House*, just with more cowboy boots.

I have no doubt that my dad and his brothers were the scourge of the entire state of Oklahoma, with fecal chili likely among the mildest of their antics. But to me, an anxious kid desperate for a label, my dad's stories were stories of belonging. They were stories of secret handshakes, of willingly branding oneself, of thrilling rivalries with the house across the street. Greek life was a real-life Sorting Hat, the *Cosmo* personality quiz to end all personality quizzes. I reasoned that, in joining a sorority, I'd be sorted into a category that would define me, blessedly, for the rest of my life. I'd land exactly where I was meant to land, supernaturally assigned a group of sisters perfectly tailored to shepherd me into the kind of adult I wanted to be.

I was kidding myself. For one thing, if you're capable of behaving even semi-normally in a public setting, you can cheat the sorority recruitment machine. I was raised by cosmetologists and am, thus, an excellent conversationalist. I had also done rigorous research into my chosen sorority's values and mission statement, which I easily snuck into conversation with the sisters. ("What am I looking for in a sorority? Oh, I'd say personal and intellectual growth, as well as philanthropic service to others!")

Given my history of cheating personality tests, it's no wonder that I cheated the Greek system. I went into recruitment knowing precisely which group I wanted to join, informed by my first few days on campus. It was easy to see which group had the largest percentage of fun hotties. It was the "Hollaback Girl" dilemma all over again. Was I a Hollaback Girl? No—but if I could cheat the system, maybe I could *become one.*

My sorority experience was fine. I got hammered a lot, leading troupes of mildly concerned classmates on drunken fraternity vandalism missions. One such mission ended with me nude save for a giant foam cowboy hat, hiking sandals, and a tiny pair of men's running shorts. I woke up the next day to discover a small chip in my tooth from falling off a raised deck, before rolling over to see my roommate's naked ass hanging out of her XL twin bed. I sighed and thought to myself, *This is living.*

Still, sometimes I wonder if I cheated myself out of an enriching college experience, if such a thing exists. What would've happened if I had been more truthful—to others, but also to myself—about my personality during those first few weeks of freshman year? Would I have landed in another sorority? No sorority at all? Where would I be if I had channeled my energy into pursuing real friendships instead of pretending to be the sort of person who looks good in a monogrammed quarter-zip sweatshirt? By the time I graduated, I had no close friends in the sorority. Today, I rarely speak to my former sisters outside of the occasional Instagram DM, though I often feel jealous of the ones who stayed close. I wonder: Who would I have met if I had allowed myself the uncertainty of being unsorted?

Other sorting mechanisms are impossible to cheat. My parents lost my birth certificate years ago, a fact that left me reeling as my friends got into astrology. I fumed knowing that I'd never be able to complete my full chart without my exact birth time. Without my chart, how would I ever really *know* myself?

Eventually, my mom found my birth announcement in an old newspaper clipping. I completed my chart and discovered that I'm a Cancer rising, which I think means I cry a lot and also enjoy shellfish. I breathed a sigh of relief, embracing the joy of being categorized in a way that is fully beyond my control. There was no cheating, no lying to the celestial bodies that determined my true nature. Finally, I had an escape from the agony of choice.

Astrology hit the mainstream when I was in my early twenties, a time when my desire to be sorted felt stronger than ever. I had graduated from college and immediately dropped my sorority mania, leaving me with the strange urge to claymate a persona from scratch. I was fumbling through the working world, nauseated by the very idea of choosing a career path. I dated willy-nilly, still unsure of the type of person I was looking for. Ancient explorers used the stars to navigate the wide and wonderful world—why couldn't I?

For a while, when presented with a decision, I'd pause and consider my astrological classification. "What would a Virgo sun, Leo moon, Cancer rising do?" I'd ask, completely excusing myself from the burden of autonomy. If I chose well, I'd blame it on my sign. ("Virgos are great at operating under pressure!") If I made the wrong choice, I'd blame that on my sign, too, falling in line with my peers as we used the solar system to justify our worst characteristics. ("So sorry that my self-absorbed Leo moon made me sleep in and miss your birthday brunch.")

I never really believed in astrology. At least, not in the kind of astrology that eighteen-year-old influencers screech about while shuffling pastel tarot decks purchased from Amazon. Oddly enough, I do sort of believe in destiny. Maybe it's because I'm naive enough to believe that my life will work out the way it's supposed to; maybe it's because, though I've long since stopped cheating on *Cosmo* personality quizzes, I still crave the feeling of having my fate dictated by some large, monolithic blob outside of myself.

At twelve, I leaned into personality tests because I was overwhelmed by the paths I saw before me. The feeling hasn't gone away. It's hard to decide what kind of person to be, and even harder to keep on deciding every day. You have to decide if you're the kind of person who wakes up at 6 a.m. for a jog or the kind of person who throws their alarm clock across the room and screams "I AM A BABY AND I WILL REST!" You have to decide if you're brave enough to join a coworker's book club or if you'd rather spend your evening searching WebMD for "brittle toenail—bad sign?" You have to decide if you're charitable, or impatient, or a messy mix of both. You have to make choices that steer you toward the kind of person you want to be, even when those choices are confusing or uncomfortable or heartbreaking. You have to be your own Eggdicator.

Sometimes, scrolling through social media, I'll shake my head in my best imitation of a curmudgeonly ISTJ. Pop psychology has taken the place of the *Cosmo* personality quiz; where I once shaped my entire personality around ultimate summer jam, internet strangers are now claiming hyperspecific classifications gathered from a tattered Psych 201 textbook.

I get it. I get the impulse to define yourself strictly as the bearer of an undiagnosed personality disorder or as a former gifted child too riddled by academic trauma to remember friends' birthdays. It's freeing to slot ourselves into categories that strip us of agency, suggesting that our worst traits are inevitable because of one's status as an Enneagram four or a Scorpio moon or, God forbid, an empath. It's tempting to seek introspection via an established set of external criteria. We're faced with more paths than ever—more possibilities with less time to explore—which explains why we've turned away from ultimate summer jams and turned toward deeper, more serious-minded forms of pigeonholing. We're also lonely. We want to find our people.

But slotting ourselves into little tubes—astrological signs, personality quiz results, social and professional labels, even fandoms—is a grave oversimplification. Lingering within our tidy tubes allows us to ignore those less tidy aspects of our personalities. We reject the idea of containing multitudes because containing multitudes is exhausting—especially for perfectionists like me, who feel pressure to perform each multitude perfectly. It's uncomfortable to sit with yourself as a nuanced thing: a fuzzy cluster of good and bad and confusing traits all stitched together in one lopsided being. We'd rather claim some external classification to explain ourselves away.

I still like personality tests. I still crave the kind of tidy, decisive self-diagnosis that accompanies Twitter psychology. I want promises—guarantees, or at least informed predictions to help guide my choices. I'd love to be plunked onto the Eggdicator and well and truly sorted, sent down one of only two possible paths. Instead, I'm left stumbling through a dark, cavelike world, forced to make choices and often choosing wrong. I have to remind myself that it's better than the alternative. To place myself inside a single tube of identity makes it impossible to change my mind, to decide what kind of person I want to be in real time. It makes it impossible to change meaningfully, to switch the radio station and choose a different Ultimate Summer Jam. To slot myself into a single, all-encompassing category blinds me to possibility—to the exhilarating idea that I can be many things—some good, some bad, some completely inconsequential—all at once.

Not long ago, I revisited *Cosmo* personality quizzes. The fat monthly issues of my sleepover days are long gone, along with the Hearst magazine chain's robust editorial budget. Instead, I found the quizzes deep in *Cosmo*'s website, a digital relic of what once was. I clicked on the first quiz, hoping to achieve some long-lost self-actualization. The title read: Does This Sexy Body Part Belong to Luke, Liam, or Chris Hemsworth? I slammed my laptop shut and screamed a cuss, scaring my beagle. Today, I am a Bad Egg. Tomorrow, I may be better.

Madison Forever

Y ou're too old to have an imaginary friend," hisses my imaginary friend, scuttling demonlike across my ceiling in her ultra-low-rise patchwork jeans. I glance up at her and shake my head, turning back to my laptop. "I'm on a deadline."

She swoops down to my eye level, sticks her finger in her mouth, and jams it into my right ear, delivering an ice-cold spectral swirly. I huff and swat her away, rolling my eyes as she flits across my desk leaving a trail of Victoria's Secret Love Spell body spray in her wake. I narrow my eyes, strike a match, and light a candle to mask the stench. Madison grins impishly, sticking her tongue out and floating back up to the ceiling.

She completes a few dreamy laps around my home office before I throw my hands up in exasperation. I uncap my purple glitter lava lamp, purchased two decades ago from a now-defunct Spencer's Gifts, and gesture toward the goo within. "Get in," I demand.

Madison crosses her arms and shakes her head, turning her back to me with a bratty pop of her hip. "If you get in, we can watch reruns of *Charmed* after work," I sigh. Madison turns around slowly.

"You promise?"

I nod, pointing again at the lava lamp. A broad smile spreads across her face as she dives, genie-like, into the lamp's glittery depths.

This is how I deal with Madison, that imaginary bully left over from my Y2K girlhood. When she first appeared, I assumed I'd have bested her by thirty, stepping into my power as a sure-footed and undeniably glamorous adult. Alas, Madison is still here, piping up to remind me of the personal failings I've yet to remedy.

She's been here all along. She sat next to me in high school biology class, taunting me for misunderstanding mitochondrial function. She joined me in college, tricking me into subsisting on eggs for three days in an attempt to achieve some arbitrary body weight. "NOTHING TASTES AS GOOD AS SKINNY FEELS," she screeched as I gagged on my tenth hard-boiled egg of the day. She perched atop my office-issued computer as I entered the professional realm, swinging her legs and insisting that I'd never be taken seriously by the executive directors of the world. She flew circles around my head, shrinking herself Tinkerbell-sized and insisting I do the same.

Now here we are, weathering the Y2K nostalgia movement together. I was naive to think that Madison would slip into oblivion along with other relics of the early 2000s, buried beneath a junkyard trash heap of long-lost Neopets passwords and spoiled SlimFast shakes. If the Urban Outfitters window display is to be believed—ultra-wide-leg skater jeans, tie-front crop tops, skeletal models, and all—everything old really is new again.

I've evolved since Madison made her circa 2004 debut. In a way, so has she; now she buys her belly chains from sullen teens on Depop and knows not to waste time on frozen Smart Ones desserts. Like me, she sports tidy frown lines etched of disillusionment and bad takeout. We both grind our teeth at night. Oddly, I don't feel as spiteful toward her as I did twenty years ago. In resolving to forgive myself for past transgressions—transgressions of the obsessive-compulsive variety, and of the bad-relationship variety, of the mean-spirited-sister variety, of the pants-shitting variety—I've resolved to soften toward Madison, that trendy, sulking monster of my own creation. I've softened toward her just as I've softened toward all my selves, those distinct spiky shapes I've taken in my frenzied attempts at being everybody's favorite.

I know I'll never banish Madison. I can't claim to have overcome my insecurities in one sweeping act of introspection. That's boring at best; at worst, it's self-delusion. Claiming complete actualization feels like selling tickets to a sideshow act. Behold, the woman who's completely overcome every layer of self-doubt and chronic people pleasing. Please do not photograph or feed.

Anyway, it's not as though Madison sprang out of nothing. She wasn't magicked into place by some dark puberty wizard. She didn't crawl out of a nightmare, nor did she burst out of my parents' attic in a cloud of dust. She was formed deliberately, a gollum shaped by fashion rags and parental expectations and gospel music and my own insecurities, some more valid than others. I remember this when she's at her worst, stomping through my home like a disgruntled parade marshal leading a procession of my deepest anxieties. My insecurities and perfectionistic tendencies are as much a part of me as anything. I can work to remedy them while still acknowledging that, like Madison, they'll likely stick around.

So, yes, Madison's still here, representing the parts of myself I'd most like to ignore. I've realized that even those parts are worthy of a little self-deprecating warmth—the occasional joke to poke fun at the embarrassing things that happen when you try to please the entire world all at once. Am I obsessed with myself? No—but I'm not entirely shrouded in shame, either. I'm somewhere in between, the product of an era designed to topple girls like me. I remain untoppled, if occasionally sheepish and regretful. For me, that's enough.

Sometimes, I allow Madison to join me on the couch. I imagine her lowering herself from the corner of the ceiling, fretting with a phantasmal Tamagotchi on the way down. I see her exhale as she lands with a soft puff on the couch cushion. She settles in; we split a bag of Ruffles and spinach dip. She double-dips and props her feet up on my lap. I groan and roll my eyes, flipping through the channels until I decide on a rerun of *Charmed*. Season 2, Episode 14: The witches travel back in time to face mistakes from their past lives. "I like this one," she murmurs sleepily. I glance at her and nod. "Me too."

ACKNOWLEDGMENTS

To the mean farm kids at the barn swings off Highway 65: Without you, I never would've learned to grit my teeth and leap from hay bales with a can of orange soda in one hand and an emaciated cat in the other, a worn leather strap the only thing between me and death or permanent disfigurement.

To my brother, a curator of fine wines and hobbit lore, and my sister, a curator of fine memes. To my mom and dad, who always have Special K Chocolatey Delight in the pantry when I come home.

To Hope Suffelette, Hannah Brashers, Ally Jeppsen, Claire Porter, and anyone else who has ever listened to me yodel via iPhone voice memo when I was supposed to be writing this book. To Emily Callen: Thank you for so many Tuesdays, and many more to come. To Cara Smith, Patty Terhune, and Michelle Golonka: Thank you for sitting cross-legged in my living room in Chicago, the greatest city on Earth. Thank you for making this place home.

To my wonderful agent, Hannah Brattessani, who can put away buffalo chicken pierogies with the best of them and always sounds so calm and collected on the phone whether the news is very good or very bad. To Peter Kispert, for taking a chance on my disgusting book proposal. To Kate Napolitano, for listening patiently when I expressed feelings of EXTREME LITERARY TERROR AND ANGUISH. To Anna Montague, for takin' us home, baby.

To Caitlin Kunkel and the satire writing community, the nerdy club of my dreams. To Johnny Morris, the founder of Bass Pro Shops: Thank you for the ducks. To Hillshire Farms, for those salami snack packs. To the inventor of waffle irons: Hats off to you!

To Archie, Turtle, Duffy, Piper, Minnie, Frankie, Sparky, Tuesday, and every other little pet who has nuzzled me as I am screaming in fear writing this book.

To the anonymous patron who placed a check for several million dollars in my mailbox, along with the key to a lavish Rhode Island seaside mansion. (Is this how manifesting works?)

SEAN: WHEN YOU READ THIS, GIVE ME KISS.

Stinky girls, highly conspicuous girls, Ozarks girls with walnut-stained hands, dizzyingly medicated girls: I hold you tight.

And to a select few individuals who I hope eat tons and tons of shit, including: my first landlord, for leaving that Leonard Cohen cassette tape in my underwear drawer; the president of my high school's chapter of Fellowship of Christian Athletes, for demanding that I send him a pic of me in my plaid padded bra when I was fourteen; the British royal family, for the evil stuff; the BTK Killer, for the killing; any of my friends that are prettier than me. Eat shit, eat shit, eat shit!

Lillian Stone lives in Chicago with her beagle. They both scream constantly.